A Practical Approach
to Performance
Interventions
and Analysis

A Practical Approach to Performance Interventions and Analysis

50 Models for Building a High-Performance Culture

Gene E. Fusch
Richard C. Gillespie

Vice President, Publisher: Tim Moore
Associate Publisher and Director of Marketing: Amy Neidlinger
Executive Editor: Jeanne Glasser Levine
Editorial Assistant: Pamela Boland
Operations Specialist: Jodi Kemper
Assistant Marketing Manager: Megan Graue
Cover Designer: Alan Clements
Managing Editor: Kristy Hart
Project Editor: Anne Goebel
Copy Editor: Gayle Johnson
Proofreader: Kathy Ruiz
Indexer: Angie Bess Martin
Compositor: Nonie Ratcliff
Manufacturing Buyer: Dan Uhrig

© 2012 by Gene E. Fusch and Richard C. Gillespie
Publishing as FT Press
Upper Saddle River, New Jersey 07458

FT Press offers excellent discounts on this book when ordered in quantity for bulk purchases or special sales. For more information, please contact U.S. Corporate and Government Sales, 1-800-382-3419, corpsales@pearsontechgroup.com. For sales outside the U.S., please contact International Sales at international@pearsoned.com.

Company and product names mentioned herein are the trademarks or registered trademarks of their respective owners.

Printed in the United States of America

First Printing May 2012

ISBN-10: 0-13-304050-X
ISBN-13: 978-0-13-304050-0

Pearson Education LTD.
Pearson Education Australia PTY, Limited.
Pearson Education Singapore, Pte. Ltd.
Pearson Education Asia, Ltd.
Pearson Education Canada, Ltd.
Pearson Educación de Mexico, S.A. de C.V.
Pearson Education—Japan
Pearson Education Malaysia, Pte. Ltd.

Library of Congress Cataloging-in-Publication Data

Fusch, Gene, 1954-
  A practical approach to performance interventions and analysis : 50 models for building a high-performance culture / Gene Fusch, Richard Gillespie.
      p. cm.
  Includes bibliographical references.
  ISBN 978-0-13-304050-0 (hbk. : alk. paper)
  1. Organizational effectiveness. 2. Performance. 3. Management. I. Gillespie, Richard C. II. Title.
  HD58.9.F87 2013
  658.3'128--dc23
                            2012006734

We dedicate this book to our wives,
Patricia Fusch and JoAnn Gillespie.
Without their support and encouragement,
this book would have remained
a concept in our minds.

Contents

Acknowledgments

We would like to begin by acknowledging our executive editor, Jeanne Glasser, as well as our project editor, Anne Goebel, and copy editor, Gayle Johnson. Because of their attention to detail and valuable suggestions, this book is truly a masterpiece.

Our university affiliations, our students, our colleagues, and professional associations such as the International Society for Performance Improvement and the American Society for Training and Development played important roles through our research and development of the models in this book. In particular, we would like to thank our good friend Marilyn Gilbert, who shared the behavioral engineering model developed by her late husband, Thomas Gilbert, which became the foundation for human performance improvement.

We also would like to thank all our clients through the years who helped us research and perfect our performance improvement methods and the Work/Life Approach. In particular, we would like to thank Gerry Kingen, founder of the Red Robin and Salty's restaurant chains and current CEO of Salty's; W. Lennox Scott, CEO of John L. Scott Real Estate Corporation; Claude Blackburn, former CEO of Dri-Eaz Products; and Sam Herring, CEO of Intrepid Learning.

About the Authors

Dr. Gene E. Fusch's career has spanned both business and education. He has conducted research on performance effectiveness and has linked theory to real-world practice. He also has helped business school students reach their educational goals. As a leadership and organizational performance consultant, he has helped many organizations with performance improvement initiatives. His clients have included Alcoa-Intalco Works, ARCO, AT&T Cable Systems, Boeing, British Petroleum, Dri-Eaz Products, Georgia-Pacific, Hexcel Interiors, Multi-Care Healthcare Systems, National Transportation Training Directors, TOSCO Refinery, Washington State Department of Transportation, Whatcom EMS, US West Communications, and Yahoo!.

Richard C. Gillespie helps organizations realize their desired end results with leadership audits, change management initiatives, and financial turnarounds. Gerry Kingen, founder of the Red Robin and Salty's restaurant chains and current CEO of Salty's, calls Gillespie "master of the obvious" because of his ability to provide succinct and straightforward Work/Life Approaches to resolve complex business needs. Some of his clients have included Lutheran Universities and Colleges, the U.S. Forest Service, Weyerhaeuser, and John L. Scott Real Estate Corporation. In addition to consulting, Gillespie has served as president of Dri-Eaz Products and Chief Operations Officer for Salty's Seafood Restaurants.

Preface

Throughout our careers we have worked with numerous organizations and people to enhance their performance and success and help them attain their desired end results. To help you improve human performance at work or at home, the American Society of Training and Development (ASTD) and the International Society for Performance Improvement (ISPI) provide excellent human performance improvement models. Likewise, many excellent writers provide good examples and models to reduce the performance gap—the gap between desired end results and reality.

Gilbert (2007) provided a foundational model for human competence that many human performance technologists have expanded upon. Indeed, Binder (2009) built upon Gilbert's model to develop his Six Boxes approach to human performance. Stolovitch and Keeps (2004, 2006) in their popular works *Performance Ain't Training* and *Beyond Telling Ain't Training* built upon this performance improvement work. They have helped numerous organizations think about performance improvement rather than training for business challenges.

These pioneers, among others in human performance technology, have shown that enhancing the workplace culture can lead to performance improvement and the desired end results. An organizational leader often faces two challenges: what to do after a successful performance improvement initiative, and how to maintain an ongoing performance improvement culture.

Begin with the end results in mind:

- Envision a place where people strive for continuous improvement.
- Envision a place where people communicate clearly.
- Envision a place where people freely share information.

- Envision a place where people understand one another.

- Envision a place where people feel that they make a difference.

- Envision a place where people respect those they work for.

- Envision a place where people want to spend their time.

- Envision a place where people have fun every day.

- Envision a place where people share the rewards both financially and emotionally based on their contribution.

In our study of a company "dedicated to creating a positive working environment through encouraging fun and enthusiasm, sharing rewards and success, being honest, fair, and productive, committing to achieve ever higher levels of excellence, promoting personal and professional growth, behaving in ways that express value and respect for everyone," we found that the Work/Life Approach helps "create an environment in which all the people, employees, associates are working towards continuous quality improvement" (Caroline, personal communication, February 15, 2001) (Fusch 2001a, p. 81–82). Moreover, the organization enjoyed an "extraordinary workplace environment. People smile. It is an amazing thing" (Caroline, personal communication, February 15, 2001) (Fusch 2001a, p. 146–147).

This book provides clear step-by-step techniques and examples to help you create and sustain a workplace that fosters continuous performance improvement. Beginning with the desired end results, we build upon the work of Gilbert, Binder, Mager, and others to provide a successful model that analyzes business problems, identifies performance gaps, determines initiatives, and measures results. Then we share our Work/Life Approach as a performance intervention bringing about a positive impact on workplace cultures, organizational performance, and people's lives.

The foundation for this book comes from our professional careers in helping numerous organizations create a performance culture (a living endowment) and from our publications such as *Managing Is*

Everybody's Business (Gillespie, 1992) and *Work/Life and the Work-place* (Fusch, 2001a). This book provides practical, commonsense methods and ideas and suggests universal knowledge based on life experiences:

- The unique Work/Life Approach to managing people and one-self provides ideas that are useful for small, medium, and large businesses.

- The Work/Life Approach is designed to help businesses stay focused on their core values and to develop a healthy working culture that drives the company toward a vision of excellence.

- Work/Life fosters the idea that all businesses are in business to acquire wealth so that they can gain additional capital to grow and prosper and do so in Valuing Ways.

- Work/Life acknowledges that all people have their own social, economic, political, and spiritual beliefs, resulting in ongoing opportunities for both unity and diversity in normal, everyday interactions at home and work.

- The Work/Life Approach provides a set of Working Beliefs that foster unity without conformity and diversity without division, regardless of religion, race, creed, color, sex, or age.

- Helping businesses stay focused on their core Working Beliefs creates a healthy workplace when all is well and when it seems like nothing is as it should be.

- The Work/Life Approach deals with the fact that people can't separate the work they do to make a living from activities/relationships outside of their work. (We take our work home and take our home to work.)

- The same is true of bringing work elements into family life.

- The Work/Life Approach helps you deal with the reality that the diversity of these beliefs in the business working environment, in the home, and in the public arena ranges from harmony to chaos.

- The Work/Life Approach steps outside of these areas and provides a set of Working Beliefs that have the potential to foster a workplace that allows people to work together regardless of their differing social, economic, political, and spiritual beliefs.

All the chapters in this book work interdependently. In addition, each chapter stands alone as a ready resource for handling situational problems, possibilities, and unique circumstances. As you read this book and ponder the Work/Life ideas in light of your specific situation, ask yourself this question: If I do not accept these ideas, what is the alternative?

1

Creating a Living Endowment for Ensuring Performance

This book describes techniques to create a workplace where members of an organization continuously strive for performance improvement. Creating such a workplace often leads to dynamic leadership, empowerment, personal ownership, and a place where people want to be every day (Fusch, 2001a). Before we focus on techniques to create a feeling of utopia in the workplace, we'll discuss organizational performance from a human performance improvement perspective. Human performance has been at the forefront of many organizations in recent years. Dr. Thomas F. Gilbert (2007), who is referred to as the father of human performance technology, pointed out the significance of human performance to the organization through his Human Competence Model, shown in Figure 1.1.

Gilbert (2007) found two main factors affected human performance in the workplace: *environmental issues* and *worker behavior*. In Gilbert's Human Competence Model, environmental opportunities for improvement are above the horizontal center line, and worker behavior opportunities for improvement are below the line. We adapted Gilbert's model to clarify that environmental opportunities for improvement above the line fall under what we will call the *hard side* of management. Worker behavior opportunities for improvement below the line fall under what we will call the *soft side* of management. It is clear from viewing Gilbert's model that the hard side of management (above the line) deals with issues that can be changed by management decisions and changes in the workplace environment. It is also evident that worker behavior on the soft side of management (below the line) is under the worker's control.

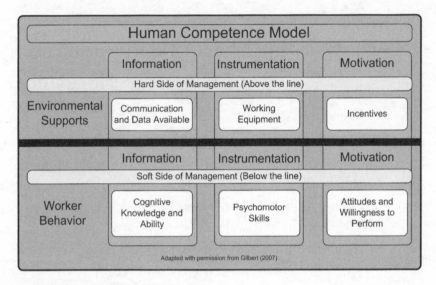

Figure 1.1 Human Competence Model

Gilbert (2007) further defined three subcategories for Environmental Supports and Worker Behavior: *information, instrumentation,* and *motivation.* Gilbert identified Information on the hard side of management as communication, data, and information available to the worker when needed to optimize workplace performance. Likewise, Gilbert defined Information on the soft side of management as the worker's knowledge and ability to take useful information and effectively perform required tasks.

In his second subcategory, Instrumentation, Gilbert described the hard side of management as having effective ergonomically correct working conditions and equipment to maximize workplace performance. The notion of effective instrumentation in the workplace environment has been evident ever since Elton Mayo's experiments at Western Electric Company's Hawthorne Works from 1927 to 1932. Mayo studied the effects of changing the physical work environment and adjusting work schedules. The changes resulted in a motivational effect not only for Mayo's test group, but also for externalities of the teams who emulated the test group on their own initiative (Mayo, 1949). Given that we have adequate instrumentation above the line, Gilbert (2007) noted that workers need the psychomotor abilities and skills on the soft side of management to perform a task.

In his third subcategory, Motivation, Gilbert pointed out that on the hard side of management, workers need motivation and incentives to want to perform. He noted that this needed to go beyond the basic monetary salary for workers to willingly perform at their best. It is interesting that Gilbert's final subcategory, Motivation, is on the soft side of management and is totally within the worker's control. *Workers have total power over their behavior to perform in the workplace.* However, any change, good or bad, above or below the line in any of the subcategories influences worker behavior to perform in the workplace. Gilbert's (2007) model provided a scientific framework to analyze worker behaviors and encouraged organizational leaders to look beyond training as the cure-all for lack of desired workplace performance.

Likewise, Binder (2009) worked to put a pragmatic "how-to" spin on Gilbert's work in what he coined Six Boxes. Boxes 1 through 3 are above the line (the hard side of management), and boxes 4 through 6 are below the line (the soft side of management). Binder argues that if you influence the first five boxes, box six will take care of itself. If you fail to influence the first five boxes, box six will be a chronic problem.

Indeed, box six (worker behavior) is paramount to workplace performance. Considerable research has been conducted on motivation, leadership influence, and why people decide to perform at a particular level. At a foundational level, Maslow (1970) maintained that the individual has needs, wants, and desires that, if left unfulfilled, may hinder self-esteem and self-actualization. On the surface, Maslow's findings make sense. People do have different levels of needs and fulfillment, and people in Western organizations tend to identify with their work. Think of one of the first icebreaker questions people use at social events when meeting someone new: "What do you do?" However, Maslow's hierarchy of human needs may fall short in motivating a worker to perform to a higher level.

Enhancing worker motivation and behavior in box six may be better illustrated by Vroom's expectancy-valence theory. It states that workers believe that performing will have certain desirable consequences (expectancy) and that they perceive their performance as a means to satisfy their needs (valence) (Vroom, 1959; Vroom, 1964; Mathieu and Martineau, 1997). Vroom further found that a worker's aroused motivation to perform was a "multiplicative function of strength of motive, the value of the incentive offered in the situation, and the expectancy that the acts will lead to the attainment of the incentive" (1959, p. 66).

As we influence the first five boxes with apparent incentives through information, instrumentation, or motivation, we affect the worker's attitude toward workplace performance. Building on Gilbert's (2007) Human Competence Model, let's look at a comprehensive organizational approach to performance.

Organizational Performance

In our ever-changing global economy, organizational leaders are striving to enhance workplace performance. With the realization that training is not always the best answer, the organizational performance profession began focusing on results-based interventions that are linked to the organization's strategic and operational plans. As a response to global competition in the past few decades, numerous academic and industry studies found that U.S. business focused primarily on activities instead of end results. One good example in the 1980s was the American automotive industry response to a loss in market share to the Japanese. It led to studying the organizational structure of the Japanese enterprise and a shift in focus toward performance improvement initiatives with measurable end results (Morgan, 1986; Nonaka & Takeuchi, 1995).

Following the trend toward focusing on performance improvement and measurable end results, human performance technologists supported by the International Society for Performance Improvement (ISPI) and the American Society for Training and Development (ASTD) began developing performance improvement approaches to help organizations improve workplace performance. We took into consideration current and past performance improvement strategies such as Gilbert (2007), Binder (2009), ISPI, ASTD, and other leaders in the performance industry. We recognized the critical need to integrate performance measurement, *real-time strategic and operational managing*, with the understanding that all businesses are in business to acquire wealth to gain additional capital to grow and prosper. This includes the absolute necessity of doing so *in Valuing Ways*. Our performance improvement model, shown in Figure 1.2, provides a comprehensive approach to analyzing the organization.

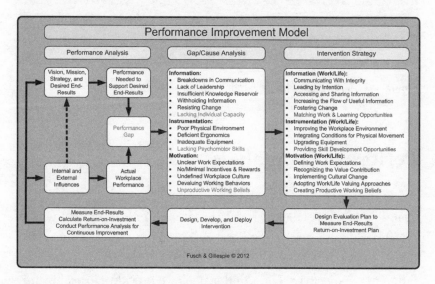

Figure 1.2 Performance improvement model

Our performance improvement model includes the organization's directions and movements, its end results, and the gap between its desired end results and its actual performance in both what is going well and what is not going well. We call this the *performance gap*. This chapter navigates each step of our model: performance analysis, gap/cause analysis, intervention selection, evaluation planning, implementation, and measuring end results (see Figure 1.3). The following chapters focus on continuous improvement for what is going well. They describe interventions to reduce the performance gap with practical, proven, how-to strategies that we call Work/Life Approaches.

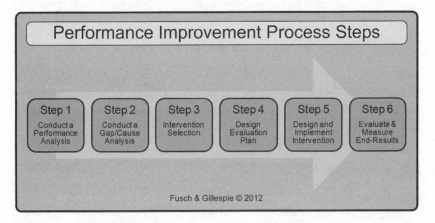

Figure 1.3 Performance improvement process steps

Performance Analysis

Performance Analysis emerges from the needs assessment to analyze what is needed to meet the desired end results. Organizational performance requires a holistic vision of what makes an effective organization rather than ideas pieced together by managers with different perspectives. Later in this book we provide a logical picture of the elements of an effective organization. We begin by identifying a clear vision, mission, strategy, and goals (desired end results) for the organization. After we have a clear expectation of these points (who we are, what we do, and where we want to go), we identify what workplace performance is needed to support our desired end results. One of our favorite questions to ask when discussing an intervention is "How will we know when we get there?" Indeed, how *will* we know when we have met the desired end results? What performance will we need to realize our desired end results?

This is often not as easy as it sounds. Frequently we have visionary leaders who develop a great vision, mission, strategy, and end results but fall short in implementation. Likewise, all too often we have great operational leaders who have difficulty looking at the organization from a visionary perspective. This leaves either unclear performance expectations to support the desired end results or performance expectations with no clear idea of whether the end results are the best ones for the organization. Long before we deploy any intervention, we need to know what performance will be needed. The following analogy offers an example for a company called Western Boats.

Western Boats

Western Boats currently manufactures 40 54-foot pleasure yachts each year. Company leadership found from a recent market analysis that people like their craft. With the proper strategy, the company could increase its market share. With this in mind, the company president sat down with senior leaders and stakeholders to develop a new vision, revise their mission, and develop a marketing strategy that would increase sales to 100 54-foot pleasure yachts per year. To meet this desired end result, performance must extend beyond the marketing and sales departments to affect the entire organization. Answering the following questions will help clarify the performance needs to support the desired end results at Western Boats:

- What performance is needed by the marketing team? How do we know when that level of performance is being reached?

- What performance is needed by the sales team? How do we know when that level of performance is being reached?
- What performance is needed by the shipping department? How do we know when that level of performance is being reached?
- What performance is needed by the production floor? How do we know when that level of performance is being reached?
- What performance is needed by the purchasing department? How do we know when that level of performance is being reached?
- What performance is needed by the inventory control warehouse? How do we know when that level of performance is being reached?
- What performance is needed by the billing department? How do we know when that level of performance is being reached?
- What performance is needed by the business office? How do we know when that level of performance is being reached?

It sounds simple and yet complex. The key is to determine at the individual, team, department, division, and organization levels what performance is needed to support desired end results. We introduce some of these methods later when we cover evaluation. Our experience has shown that each workplace environment has specific issues and concerns that must be addressed. We recommend using scientific methods to analyze each organizational environment. These may include qualitative research methods (focus groups, project teams, ad hoc committees, interviews, observations, questionnaires), quantitative research methods (performance indicators, production records, trend analysis, surveys, questionnaires), or a combination.

After we identify clear expectations for the needed performance, we identify and measure the actual level of workplace performance. This performance has a cause-and-effect relationship from internal and external influences. We examine these influences during a gap/ cause analysis. At this point, we spend our effort identifying the actual performance indicators and perform a basic mathematics problem, as shown in our Performance Analysis Model (see Figure 1.4). The level of the needed performance for desired end results minus the actual workplace performance equals our performance gap.

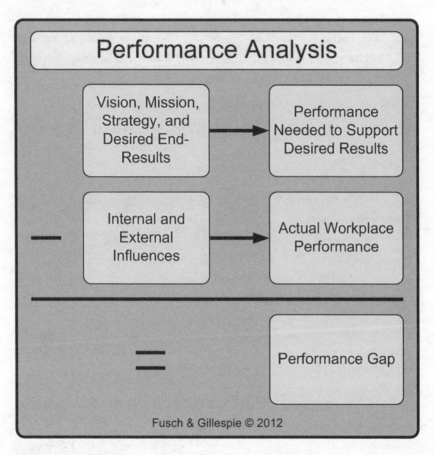

Figure 1.4 Performance Analysis Model

A systematic performance analysis need not take a lot of time, yet it should do the following:

- Analyze the organization's vision, mission, strategy, and desired end results.

- Link the desired performance to support the organizational strategic business plan.

- Determine a methodology to measure when the desired performance has been met.

- Analyze the internal and external environment. External factors could include economic conditions, competition, and customer and vendor relations. Internal issues could include equipment and technology, breakdowns in communication, resistance to change, and labor-management issues. All or only some of these considerations could be included.

- Link workforce performance with the environment.

- Determine the gap between the desired performance and the actual performance.

Western Boats, Part 2

Returning to our Western Boats analogy, it currently takes the laminating division 6.3 manufacturing days to lay up and fabricate a fiberglass hull. This equates to 40 hulls per year. The leadership's desired end result is to produce one hull every 2.52 manufacturing days. Thus, a gap of 3.78 manufacturing days exists between the current timeframe of 6.3 manufacturing days and the needed performance of 2.52 manufacturing days.

2.52 manufacturing days (Desired Performance)

–6.3 manufacturing days (Actual Performance)

<3.78> manufacturing days (Performance Gap)

We need to identify the cause of the performance gap. Western Boats probably has performance gaps in more areas than just the laminating division that limit the company's production output. However, this example helps simplify the performance analysis.

Gap/Cause Analysis

We have done the math and found that a gap exists between the performance needed to support the desired end results and the state of the actual workplace performance. Unfortunately, in the past, many organizations failed to analyze the cause of performance gaps. Some turned to training as a performance cure-all, and others ignored the cause of gaps. Gilbert (2007) found that managers frequently requested training when training was not the answer to improving human performance. Often we hear workers say something like "They sent me to (the same) training three times. But I already know how to do my job!" Robert Mager (Mager & Pipe, 1997), one of the early performance professionals, became well known for his gun test: If I put a gun to my subordinate's head, will he or she still be unable to perform as I would like? At the time, Mager was working with the military, which probably could relate to Mager's gun analogy. Strategic performance and training game developer Dr. Sivasailam Thiagarajan (aka Thiagi) came up with a more proactive example: If you ask someone if he could perform a task for a million dollars, and he says he could, it is not a knowledge or skill deficiency—it is a motivational deficiency. As we discussed with Gilbert's (2007) Human Competence Model, all too often the idea that training would "fix" people missed the mark when the cause of the gap was unrelated to worker knowledge or skills.

When it comes to identifying the performance gap, we must ask some key questions:

- What business indicators will we use to measure the performance?
- What performance is needed to create the desired end results?
- What is the actual performance?

- What leading causes are creating the gap between the desired performance and actual performance?
- Are the leading causes of the performance gap related to information, instrumentation, or motivational challenges?
- What will happen if we do nothing?

These questions help you analyze the causes of a performance gap. With our approach, we begin by thinking about the desired end results and looking for causes that have a definitive and doable intervention linked to them. Our model, shown in Figure 1.5, provides a small sampling of causes. The next chapter discusses the Work/Life Approach, with practical and effective interventions for reducing performance gaps.

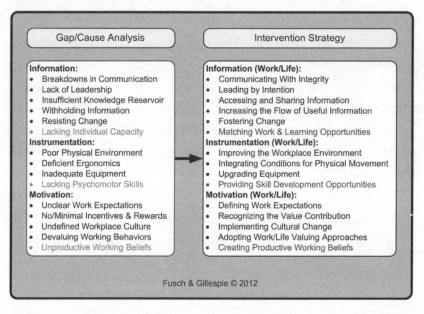

Figure 1.5 Performance gaps and intervention strategies

Here are some of the causes of performance gaps on the organization-controlled hard side of management (above the line) in the Information subcategory:

- **Breakdowns in communication.** Lack of communication systems, breakdowns in communication from individuals failing to share information, departments and teams not talking to each other, too much useless information such as e-mails sent to everybody when only a small group or specific individuals need the communication.

- **Lack of leadership.** Managers who fall short in leadership skills, leading in the wrong direction, unclear expectations, no job description or a job description that does not match the job, too many managers with opposing directives.

- **Insufficient knowledge reservoir.** Lack of a viable knowledge management system or too much information without a system to identify useful information that workers need to perform well in their jobs. Or the right information is unavailable when needed.

- **Withholding information.** Lack of useful information for the workers who need it. Security measures in place that prevent access to those who need the information. Often kept in a division, group, team, or individual vault without sharing with others who would benefit from having the information.

- **Resisting change.** Given the plethora of research on change management and the human resistance to change, this cause may represent lack of vision, lack of resources, lack of knowledge, or complacency.

The performance-gap causes on the soft side of management (below the line) in the Information subcategory likely indicate that the workers do not have the necessary knowledge or abilities or are affected by other influences that impact their ability to process information.

The performance-gap causes on the organization-controlled hard side of management in the Instrumentation subcategory may include the following:

- **Poor physical environment.** An environment where the facility causes constraints in workplace performance. May include poor climate control, inadequate lighting, poor facility layout, and safety hazards. Potential hazards and dangerous chemicals with inadequate safety protocols. Frequent injuries or haphazard regard for worker welfare.

- **Deficient ergonomics.** A workplace environment where workers must perform physical actions that may cause fatigue or injury over time.

- **Inadequate equipment.** Equipment that is poorly maintained, is not functioning properly, causes hazards to workers, and fails to provide the best return on investment (ROI) for its use.

The performance-gap causes on the soft side of management in the Instrumentation subcategory likely indicate that the workers do not have the psychomotor skills, abilities, or competence to perform their tasks.

The performance-gap causes on the organization-controlled hard side of management in the Motivation subcategory may include the following:

- **Unclear work expectations.** It is common for workers to be hired or transferred without a clearly defined job role. All too often managers do not define their expectations or communicate them to their workers.

- **No/minimal incentives and rewards.** Lack of rewards, including compliments, recognition, and appraisals identifying positive contributions. Lack of opportunity for career development or advancement. Low pay and/or lack of a benefits package. Elimination of pay, benefits, or other rewards.

- **Undefined workplace culture.** A culture that is hostile or less than desirable. A culture where you must lose yourself to conform and survive.

- **Devaluing worker behaviors.** Leadership and/or coworkers who do not value positive worker behaviors.

The performance-gap causes on the soft side of management in the Motivation subcategory likely indicate problems in any of the other management categories. This affects the workers' attitude and willingness to perform.

Every organization has specific issues and concerns that cause performance gaps. The leading scientific methods to identify performance gaps include performance indicators, direct observation, worker interviews, exit interviews, focus groups, project teams, ad hoc committees, and questionnaires. Often results are better when an impartial third party who workers are comfortable with is brought in. As we discussed, all too often organizations omit the performance and gap analysis and immediately conduct a training project to improve performance. And all too often the training strategy selected may not be related to the actual cause of the performance problem, and the intervention may have been a costly mistake. An adage summarizes this perspective: "There's never enough time to do it right, and all the time in the world to do it over" (unknown author).

It is clear that the gap/cause analysis builds on the performance analysis and determines the cause of the gap between the desired workplace performance and the actual workplace performance. The gap analysis helps determine the criteria for the best intervention to obtain the desired performance.

Intervention Strategy

There is a direct correlation between the gap/cause analysis and an intervention strategy. An intervention strategy is an opportunity for change. The most effective implementation is an effective change initiative that produces the best end result for the lowest cost. Most companies move from analysis to implementation before designing an evaluation strategy. Before we design and implement an intervention, we must first design an *evaluation/measurement/return-on-investment strategy*. This section discusses the selection and rationale for potential interventions to reduce the performance gap and prepare for the next section on evaluation and measurement.

There must be a direct link between the performance gap and the intervention strategy for the desired end results to occur:

Performance-Gap Cause	Intervention Strategy
Breakdowns in communication	Communicating with integrity
Lack of leadership	Leading by intention
Insufficient knowledge reservoir	Accessing and sharing information
Withholding information	Increasing the flow of useful information
Resisting change	Fostering change
Lacking individual capacity	Matching work and learning opportunities
Poor physical environment	Improving the workplace environment
Deficient ergonomics	Integrating conditions for physical movement
Inadequate equipment	Upgrading equipment
Lacking psychomotor skills	Providing skill development opportunities
Unclear work expectations	Defining work expectations
No/minimal incentives and rewards	Recognizing the value contribution
Undefined workplace culture	Implementing cultural change
Devaluing worker behaviors	Adopting work/life valuing approaches
Unproductive working beliefs	Creating productive working beliefs

Numerous interventions may reduce the performance gap. However, for the growth of the organization and the well-being of its employees, you must select interventions that allow the organization to accomplish the desired end results with the best ROI. As we analyze the intervention, there is value in determining the organization's strategic plan and how the intervention will impact the culture today and tomorrow. Performance improvement leaders must decide whether to use in-house resources, do outsourcing, or use custom or off-the-shelf interventions.

Similar to a supply or merchandise inventory in organizations, performance leaders use an intervention inventory to help determine the best delivery method for a specific performance intervention. Because of the diversity of organizational needs and the complexity of different approaches, we use a 21-point inventory. It takes the form of a worksheet/questionnaire and helps you decide whether to use a specific intervention:

1. What desired end results will this performance intervention address?

   What desired change does this performance intervention intend to address?

2. Is there a political rationale for using one method over another?

   This may be an issue if the company markets a specific delivery medium and using another delivery method may have systemic repercussions.

3. List any special or unique parameters specific to this project.

4. Who is the audience?

   This question includes analyzing the type of worker (diversity and cultural concerns, younger versus older workers, accounting, sales, manufacturing, technical, management).

5. Will there be time for people to participate in the intervention?

   For learning opportunities, introduction to job aids, and so on. Will supervisors release subordinates from other duties to participate?

6. Motivation to participate.

   Will the employees worry that their work will pile up while they participate in the intervention? Answering this question may identify a need to promote the intervention. (This includes everyone from senior executives to hourly workers.)

7. What are the development time and cost for the intervention?
8. Who will need to develop the intervention?
9. What will the framework look like?
10. How will the intervention be administered? Delivered?
11. Is technology in place to support this intervention?
12. What additional technology will the organization need to implement this intervention?
13. What are the constraints in deploying this intervention?
14. What are the advantages of using this particular intervention?
15. What are the disadvantages of using this particular intervention?
16. Would another implementation method work better?
17. Would another approach bring similar results for less investment?
18. Will this strategy bring the desired end results?
19. How will you measure/evaluate the outcomes?
20. Who will support this performance intervention?
21. Will the primary stakeholders buy into it?

Review the following case study of a hypothetical resort, and use the 21-point inventory to consider potential training interventions. Although this case study is limited in details and triggers more questions, it helps you conceptualize how to use the inventory for other interventions.

Last Resort

This case study describes a resort on Cape Flattery in Washington State. It stands on the most northwestern corner of the continental United States. The resort owns 20 acres of what it calls the most fantastic views in the world. For years a local family with a history in Washington State dating back to 1897 owned and operated the resort as a 42-bed lodge. In 2007, a global conglomerate purchased the resort, and a major two-year construction project followed. Recently the resort was featured on the Travel Channel as a location that the rich and famous seek out. It offers eight meeting rooms that can each hold 300 people and three large rooms that can hold 2,000 occupants. The resort has 100 plush suites, 400 view suites, and 600 economy rooms. With a kitchen staff of 40, a hotel staff of 110, a conference staff of 10, and an administrative staff of 10, the company views its 170 employees as a vital part of its goal of 95 percent occupancy year-round. The company also wants the world to view the resort as the "Ritz Carlton of the Northwest" and feel like it is a home away from home.

Performance Analysis Findings

You are brought in as a performance improvement consultant to help the resort meet its goals. In your performance analysis you note that the resort was full to capacity during the peak season in the summer months and during the April conference season. However, during the rest of the year the resort booked few conferences, and 50 to 60 percent of the rooms were unoccupied. Your analysis identifies two major concerns. First, many of the 110 hotel staff (as well as the 40 kitchen staff) are inexperienced in customer service. They seem not to realize that every customer is valuable to the organization's vision, mission, and desired end results. Second, there seems to be a skills gap in the conference marketing team— primarily in networking with large organizations and professional associations.

Intervention Selection

Although you do not have all the information and data you need to make a precise intervention selection, work through the performance inventory, and write down what you know now and what you still need to know.

The remaining chapters will provide valuable insight and dynamic interventions. They describe the Work/Life Approach to creating a performance culture that fosters continuous improvement. Now we will move on to the next step in our performance improvement model—measuring end results.

Design an Evaluation Plan to Measure End Results and Your Return on Investment

We've already discussed selecting an intervention strategy to reduce the performance gap between the needed performance to bring the desired end results and the actual workplace performance. Now we will discuss designing an evaluation measurement strategy so that you know when the desired performance has been met. This section briefly discusses scientific methods to evaluate the results of the intervention and to measure the ROI. Let's start with a brief review of the origins of measuring the ROI for performance interventions.

In the beginning, intervention evaluation was most prominent in the training classroom when evaluation was desired. Unfortunately, most training evaluation encompassed and still encompasses what performance professionals call "smiley face evaluation." This is a brief questionnaire at the end of the training session that asks the participants if they liked the course, if they liked the facility, if they liked the instructor, and if the coffee and donuts were good. In other words, did they have fun, and do they want to do it again? From a measurement perspective, such a questionnaire tells us if we have workers who like to take time away from their jobs and sit in a classroom enjoying the presentation, facility, coffee, and donuts. What we do not know is if the training intervention had a positive impact on the desired end results.

Interest is growing in results-based performance improvement interventions that are linked to the organization's strategic plan. This is visible through the interest in going beyond the traditional four steps for evaluating training programs (assessing the reaction, learning, behavior, and results) and calculating the ROI for training (Kirkpatrick, 2006; Phillips, 1997, 2011). See Figure 1.6.

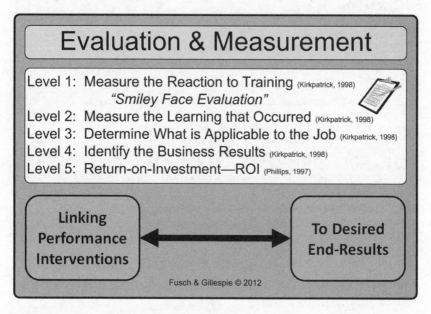

Figure 1.6 Evaluating and measuring training

We argue that an ROI strategy should always be employed before the design, development, and deployment of a performance intervention. Doing so ensures that the best intervention was selected and that the intervention is designed to bring the desired end results. Indeed, as Covey (2004) maintained that you should always begin with the end in mind, we too have always considered the desired end result before initiating any performance intervention. So to begin with the end in mind, we will walk through our five-step ROI process (see Figure 1.7).

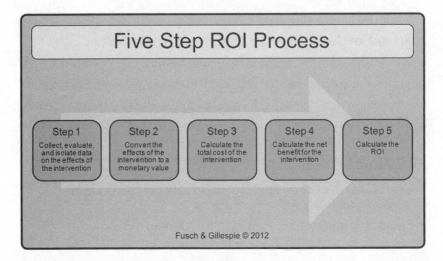

Figure 1.7 Five-step ROI process

Our ROI model involves five basic steps that seem simple yet are often complex. The following list discusses the steps and how to overcome barriers to conducting an ROI process:

1. Collect, evaluate, and isolate tangible and intangible data concerning the effects of a performance intervention.

2. Convert the isolated effects of a performance intervention into a monetary value.

3. Calculate the total cost of a performance intervention.

4. Calculate the net benefit of a performance intervention by subtracting the total performance intervention costs from the total performance intervention benefits.

5. Calculate the ROI by dividing the net performance intervention benefits from step 4 by the training program costs from step 3 and then multiplying the product by 100.

Figure 1.8 mathematically depicts the ROI process. We take the monetary value of the effects of performance intervention and subtract the cost of performance intervention to get the net benefit of performance intervention. Then we divide the net benefit of performance intervention by the total cost of performance intervention to calculate the ROI. Because we are used to looking at the ROI in percentages, we multiply the ROI by 100 to calculate the return-on-investment percentage, which we call ROI %.

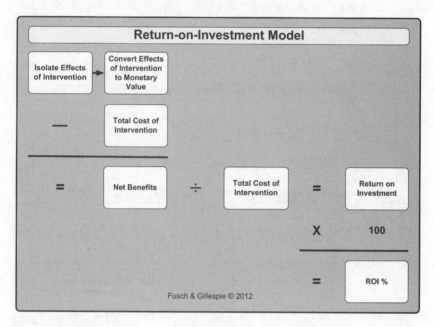

Figure 1.8 ROI model

The literature provides numerous case studies and detailed descriptions of the ROI process for determining the effectiveness of a performance intervention. As you can see from our model, the math and five-step ROI process appear linear and simple. However, sometimes distinct peculiarities hinder an organization's data collection for an ROI process. To overcome these barriers to data collection, we employ the scientific method of hypothetical-deductive reasoning to evaluate the effectiveness of the intervention. Appendix A provides more details on the methods we use to determine the program costs and to measure the effects of the performance intervention that may be used by organizations with similar issues. After we have a strategy in place to measure the desired end results, we can design, develop, and deploy the performance intervention.

Design, Develop, and Deploy the Intervention

We have analyzed our performance gap, decided on the best intervention to reduce the performance gap between the actual performance and the performance needed to obtain the desired end results, and designed a strategy to measure the performance intervention results. Now it is time to design/plan, develop/purchase, and deploy the performance intervention (see Figure 1.9).

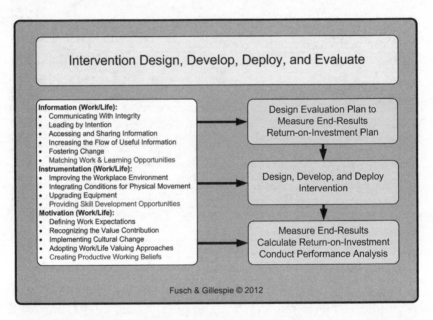

Figure 1.9 Intervention design, development, deployment, and evaluation

Reviewing our intervention selection inventory, we determine the best intervention. We figure out whether we can implement the intervention within the organization or if it would be better to purchase the services/products or partner with another organization(s) to deploy the needed intervention. At this point we implement the intervention and our measurement strategy.

Measure End Results and Calculate Return on Investment

In the Design Evaluation Plan to Measure End Results/Return on Investment step of our Performance Improvement process, we discussed how to plan and measure for ROI. At this point, while and after the performance intervention has been implemented, it is critical to measure the end results.

Perhaps more important to human performance professionals is that going beyond the basic evaluation to calculate the ROI allows you to strategically evaluate performance interventions. You also can provide management with solid information on the effects of the performance intervention vis-à-vis the company's strategic plan. Indeed, the greater concern for human performance professionals may not be whether to evaluate, but how to provide results-based data and reports to senior management to support their contribution to the organization's mission and/or strategic plan.

Conduct a Performance Analysis

In addition to identifying the ROI for the performance intervention, the comprehensive analysis provides the data for a new performance analysis to determine additional areas for performance improvement. Hence, we have come full circle. We have conducted a performance analysis, conducted a gap analysis, selected an intervention, designed an evaluation plan, designed and implemented the intervention, and conducted an ROI strategy to measure the end results.

Now that we have had a comprehensive discussion of performance improvement, we dedicate the remainder of this book to our Work/Life Approach to creating a workplace for continuous improvement with practical how-to performance interventions.

Summary

This chapter has described creating a living endowment for ensuring performance. We have discussed the critical need for integrating performance measurement, real-time strategic and operational managing, with the understanding that all businesses want to acquire wealth and gain additional capital to grow and prosper. This includes the necessity of doing so in Valuing Ways.

Our performance improvement model includes the organization's directions and movements, its end results, and the gap between its desired end results and the actual performance. This includes both what is going well and what is not. We call this the *performance gap*.

This chapter navigated each step of our model through performance analysis, gap/cause analysis, intervention selection, evaluation planning, implementation, and measuring end results.

The following chapters focus on continuous improvement for what is going well. They also provide interventions to reduce the performance gap with practical, proven how-to strategies that we call Work/Life Approaches.

Chapter 2 begins with the business results while continuously thinking about the desired end results. Chapter 2 introduces Work/Life Approaches:

- The Organizational Bill of Rights and subsequent tools provide clear direction and movement for everyone working within the organization.

- The Celestial Approach to Managing frees the people closest to the work to make decisions, identify concepts, and make dynamic decisions about everything a person or organization brings to a specific end result. Rather than using a two-dimensional hierarchy shown on an x-y axis, this approach metaphorically takes a more elliptical/celestial view. It focuses on a specific task/idea/ intent that floats through the galaxy rather than focusing on a lockstep procedural hierarchy.

- The Communication System represents a flow of work where employees do not need to go to the boss for decisions and assignments. Instead, people work together, and decisions are made closest to the action.

- Several additional tips and strategies will help you realize your desired end results.

2

Starting with the Desired End Results

When a baker begins to prepare a cake for a celebration, he or she begins with a vision of how the finished cake will look and taste. Likewise, a bricklayer starts a project with a clear vision of what the finished project will look like. For the past decades in our Work/Life Approach to managing, we have always started by identifying our desired end results (whether it is a meeting, project, performance intervention, or just a routine daily task). By identifying our end results up front, we have clear measurable indicators to help us stay focused and ensure that we accomplish what we plan to accomplish.

This chapter discusses the following Work/Life Approaches to help you focus on the desired end results in your workplace:

- Principles of the Work/Life Approach
- Organizational Bill of Rights
- The Celestial Approach to Managing
- The Communication System

Before we navigate through the different Work/Life Approaches, let's review the desired end results that these practical, commonsense methods, ideas, and tools can provide in your organization:

- The unique Work/Life Approach to managing people and oneself provides ideas that are readily useful for small, medium, and large businesses.

- The Work/Life Approach is designed to help businesses stay focused on their core values and to develop a healthy working culture that drives the company toward a vision of excellence.

- Work/Life fosters the idea that all businesses are in business to acquire wealth so that they can gain additional capital to grow and prosper and do so in Valuing Ways.

- Work/Life acknowledges that all people have their own social, economic, political, and spiritual beliefs. They result in ongoing opportunities for both unity and diversity in normal, everyday interactions at home and work.

- The Work/Life Approach provides a set of Working Beliefs that foster unity without conformity and diversity without division regardless of religion, race, creed, color, sex, or age.

- Helping businesses stay focused on their core Working Beliefs provides a healthy workplace during times when all is well and in times when it seems like nothing is as it should be.

- The Work/Life Approach deals with the fact that people can't separate the work they do to make a living from activities and relationships outside of their work. (We take our work home, and we take our home to work.)

- The same is true regarding bringing work elements into family life.

- The Work/Life Approach provides help for dealing with the reality that the diversity of these beliefs in the business working environment, in the home, and in the public arena ranges from harmony to chaos.

- The Work/Life Approach steps outside of these areas and provides a set of Working Beliefs that have the potential to foster a workplace that allows people to work together regardless of their differing social, economic, political, and spiritual beliefs.

Principles of the Work/Life Approach

The Work/Life Approach by design helps companies stay focused on their core values to develop a healthy working culture that will drive the company toward its vision of excellence. In today's global economy, people may be working from their home, car, boat, vacation cabin, or business location. More and more people cannot separate their personal life from their working life. We as a society tend to identify with what we do now more than ever. Most people work in some vocation or avocation; the only difference between people is the scope of their work. As shown in Figure 2.1, the Work/Life Approach acknowledges that in any given organization, *people are all equal in value—just the scope of their work is different.*

Figure 2.1 Work/Life Approach

In his study of a manufacturing organization that utilized the Work/Life Approach, Fusch found that the organization valued workers at all levels of the company. One production worker noted that "we are equal in status but work in a different scope" (2001a, p. 119). Throughout the organization, Fusch found that people listened to each other and did a great job of valuing each other. The company's philosophy was people-oriented, and the company cared about its associates. One associate pointed out that "there are no double standards here" (Fusch, 2001a, p. 119). Fusch (2001a) conducted interviews and meetings and observed the corporate president. In doing so, he found that the president felt passionately that the company should have a workplace that not only values people but also helps them grow in their personal and work lives.

Hence, the Work/Life Approach is founded on the fact that *people are all equal in value—just the scope of their work is different.* This approach also incorporates the basic Working Belief that people cannot separate themselves from their social, economic, political, and spiritual values and beliefs. The Work/Life Approach uses the diversity of these Working Beliefs to create a workplace that realizes the desired end results.

Organizational Bill of Rights

An organization by definition is a group of people brought together for a specific purpose, such as any small, medium, or large enterprise. Within the work organization are specific responsibilities employees have to the company and specific responsibilities that the company has to its employees. All too often these responsibilities are left unclear. The Work/Life Approach provides a detailed Organizational Bill of Rights (see Figure 2.2) and subsequent tools that offer clear direction and movement for everyone working in the organization.

Organizational Bill of Rights

Understanding and Clarification

- What people were hired to do
- The expected results of work
- How the expected results are measured
- Needed – knowledge, experience and skills
- Resources – financial, physical, time
- Regular feedback/performance reviews
- Paid for performance

Fusch & Gillespie © 2012

Figure 2.2 Organizational Bill of Rights

Understanding and Clarifying What People Were Hired to Do

It is not uncommon to see generic job descriptions that do not cover the scope of a specific worker's job. People work best when they have a clear and detailed understanding of the task they are to perform. This includes specific individuals such as a new hire, transfer, or transitioning worker, as well as a working team or group. Moreover, it's freeing to understand the work, responsibilities, authority to perform work, and process of being held accountable. It helps people create energy and helps make them more successful. *When people do not have clear roles or understand their work, they become frustrated.* In later chapters, we discuss the Working Guidelines that should be used for all job classifications, as well as groups and committees to clarify and enhance workplace performance.

Understanding and Clarifying the Expected End Results of People's Work

In addition to people understanding their scope of work, it is important that they understand the results that other people expect from them. Along with understanding the expectations for their performance, people also need to understand the performance expectations of their coworkers and partnering groups, departments, and divisions up and down the supply chain. That way, they can help maximize the work flow and performance. Future chapters will introduce several Work/Life Tools to enhance communication and understanding between people, groups, departments, and divisions in the workplace.

Understanding and Clarifying How the Expected Results Are Measured

People perform best when they have a clear understanding of the expectations and desired end results of their performance. Consider the ambiguity in the worker's understanding and the supervisor's frustration from lack of both job duties and expected end results described in the following case study. It resulted from a performance assessment at a large West Coast manufacturer. Although this case study does not give the organization's real name, the scenario is commonplace and could be happening in many organizations.

Western Enterprises Case Study

Don Juan has been working for Western Enterprises for 12 years. With only a high school education, Don started as a warehouse worker. After demonstrating competence in Microsoft Office, he worked his way up to a shipping clerk position. Eight years ago, when Don was promoted, he learned his duties on the job from other shipping clerks. Don is charismatic and seems suited for his current position. Furthermore, employees and customers seem to enjoy visiting with Don. Last year, when the department's supervisor retired, Don made a good first impression on his new boss. However, the new department supervisor soon became disenchanted with Don's performance.

The new supervisor observed that Don spent a lot of time visiting with people and seldom completed the tasks assigned to him. It seemed to take Don hours to prepare a shipping invoice. In frustration, the new supervisor asked human resources to either fire Don or transfer him to another department. Human resources responded that because all of Don's evaluations had been satisfactory, they could not just get rid of him without first offering him a professional development plan. If Don did not improve, the supervisor would need to document his poor performance in Don's evaluations over time. After another month went by, the new supervisor felt that Don needed a professional development plan and turned to the training director for help.

The supervisor told the training director that Don did not prepare shipping invoices in a reasonable amount of time and was very slow at inputting data into Microsoft Excel and Access. The supervisor stated that Don was a pleasant person but did not seem to have the skills he needed to complete his work at the shipping clerk level. To get the department performing at par, the supervisor was willing to allocate extra funds for Don's skill training.

As you reflect on this case study, you likely have unanswered questions about Don's computer skills. However, it appears that there may be a disconnect between Don's opinion of his job performance and the end results his supervisor expects. The Working Guidelines covered in Chapter 3 describe how to create a clear understanding of the expected performance and end results for a specific worker.

Understanding and Clarifying the Needed Knowledge, Experience, and Skills to Perform Well on the Job

With the rapid technological changes in today's workplace, it is imperative for the health of the organization and for the future of individual workers to keep their knowledge and skills fine-tuned. Covey (2004) provided an excellent analogy to point out the importance of fine-tuning one's skills. He described two loggers in the forest with dull saws. One logger worked hard for the better part of a day to fell a tree. The other logger spent a half hour sharpening his saw and then quickly cut down a tree. Having worked with the forest and lumber industries, we related well to this example of the value of spending time and effort sharpening one's saw (knowledge and skills).

From a monetary perspective, Gary S. Becker (1993), an economist and Nobel Prize recipient, found that there is a sequential relationship between learning and productivity. This relationship between learning and production/earnings has inspired numerous economic studies of cost-benefit analysis for different levels of education. Analyzing the costs and benefits to the individual, the research has found that the cost and time spent learning (reduced earnings while acquiring an education) result in a positive financial return on investment. (See Chapter 1 and Appendix A for additional information on ROI.) Indeed, people need to understand that the needed knowledge, skills, and experience increase their competence to perform on their jobs today and tomorrow, as well as their financial potential.

Likewise, it is imperative that the company provide opportunities for people to gain the knowledge, skills, and experience they need to continually improve their job performance. It was not long ago that we heard from our clients (and we still do), "What if we provide learning opportunities for our workers, and then they leave the company?" Today many of those same organizations are asking, "What if we don't provide learning opportunities for our workers, and they stay?" One of the highest compliments a company can be paid is when it provided professional development opportunities for its employees; an employee outgrew a current position and elected to leave to use his/ her skills and return when an opportunity became available.

It is evident that both individuals and the organization must ensure that each individual in the organization has and takes advantage of opportunities to obtain the needed knowledge, experience, and skills to perform well on their jobs.

Understanding and Clarifying the Resources Needed: Financial, Physical, and Time

People need to understand the resources needed to perform their jobs. This includes financial, physical, and time commitments. Although family and social responsibilities outside work can create challenges, unexpected absences can cripple many organizations. This highlights the one-on-one relationship between the manager and the employee in that the manager senses when the employee's personal, financial, and time commitment are impacting the work. The same is true if the financial, physical, and time commitment at work are affecting the employee's personal life.

Understanding and Clarifying to Provide and Receive Regular Feedback

Chapter 1 introduced causes of performance gaps on the organization-controlled hard side of management (above the line) in the Motivation subcategory:

- **Unclear work expectations.** It is common for workers to be hired or transferred without a clearly defined job role. All too often managers do not define their expectations or communicate them to their workers.

- **No/minimal incentives and rewards.** Lack of rewards, including compliments, recognition, and appraisals identifying positive contributions. Lack of opportunity for career development or advancement. Low pay and/or lack of a benefits package. Elimination of pay, benefits, or other rewards.

- **Undefined workplace culture.** A culture that is hostile or less than desirable. A culture where you must lose yourself to conform and survive.

- **Devaluing worker behaviors.** Leadership and/or coworkers who do not value positive worker behaviors.

To generate some critical thought about the need for clear job expectations and regular feedback, review the following case study. It introduces a specific performance problem in an organization. Although this case study does not give the organization's real name, the scenario is commonplace and could be happening in many organizations.

Eastern Manufacturing

Several years ago, during a growth initiative, Eastern Manufacturing expanded its production operations into several new markets. This required expansion in the sales, administrative, production, shipping and receiving, and customer service departments. After brief growth in production and sales and initial profit projections, the company began experiencing delivery shortages, shipping errors, and customer complaints. Concerned about image and retaining profits, the leadership developed a shipping coordinator position to act as a liaison between sales, production, and shipping. The following advertisement went out:

Help Wanted: With a recent expansion into new markets, Eastern Manufacturing has an immediate opening for shipping coordinators. Qualifications: Bachelor's degree in business, operations, or shipping, or related education or experience. Send your resume to Eastern Manufacturing, c/o Human Resources Management.

Six shipping coordinators were hired under the supervision of John Performance in the sales department. These new recruits were provided cubicles on the north end of the sales department, near the stairs to the production warehouse. Given their marching orders, these new hires worked to facilitate a smoother transition between the sales orders, the production planning, and the shipping department to ensure that customer orders were filled correctly and in a timely manner. This initial intervention helped reduce some of the company's challenges. The new shipping coordinators found that they were a valuable asset to the organization.

Within a few months, the customer service department director, who saw his job as dealing with product issues after delivery, turned over all shipping-related complaints to the shipping coordinators. Soon after, John Performance came up with an idea to increase repeat sales and take some of the burden off his sales representativevs so that they could spend more time making new customer sales. John told the shipping coordinators to contact customers after delivery to ensure that they were satisfied and to see if they needed any more products. Over the next few years the shipping coordinator duties morphed with the company's growth until there were 20 shipping coordinators. This required restructuring and forming a new department with a manager who reported to the director of sales. Under the direction of the new manager, the shipping coordinator position changed and diversified to include customer advisors and customer sales associates as well as shipping coordinators.

The interesting challenge was that most if not all of the employees were hired under the same generic shipping coordinator title and qualifications. As employees came and left, the job continued to change, and there was no adequate job description or written expectations for performance. A decade later, the department now titled Customer Relations had a wing to house the 46 personnel performing a variety of duties, including order taking, customer surveys, customer relations, and shipping assurance.

With the diversity of tasks but basically the same pay and title, performance issues began emerging. The customer relations manager had to determine the following:

- Were people doing what they were supposed to do?
- What were people supposed to do?
- What distinguishes one employee's task from another?

- How can an employee be evaluated?
- If a reduction in force were required, how could the high performers be distinguished from the low performers?
- What are the job performance expectations?

The Customer Relations department at Eastern Manufacturing would be difficult to lead. Without clear job expectations, there is no way to conduct performance evaluations. Chapter 3 introduces methods that provide clear Working Guidelines that aid in performance evaluation and improvement.

However, even when clear job descriptions and duties do exist, it is interesting how seldom adequate performance evaluations occur. A concept called *360-degree feedback* gathers input from all levels of the organization to identify what an employee is doing well and what he or she could do differently. When a company has demonstrated that it is open to sharing what people are doing well as well as suggestions for performance improvement, it is amazing to traditional hourly shop floor workers that they can share their opinions about the company. How willing are people (president, managers, supervisors, and workers) to listen to this kind of feedback? (360-degree feedback from all levels of the organization that identifies what people can continue doing and what people can do differently.) This occurs when valuing behavior is evident throughout the company and the company is open to sharing what people are doing well and also how they could improve their skills. This information is enhanced and acted on. Several case studies have shown that it is not unusual for executives working late at night to get a feel for how the company is doing (its pulse) from custodians, second-shift workers, and warehouse staff.

Understanding and Clarifying What Is Required to Be Paid for Performance

In his address to the Society of Mechanical Engineers, Frederick Taylor introduced his scientific management methods with the term "maximum prosperity." He defined this to mean "not only large dividends for the company or owner, but the development of every branch of the business to its highest state of excellence, so that prosperity may be permanent. In the same way maximum prosperity for each employee means not only higher wages than are usually received by men of this class, but, of more importance still, it means the development of each man to his state of maximum efficiency" (Taylor, 1911, p. 1). Although it appears that Taylor had good intentions, his philosophy of scientific management led to the machine metaphor, in which workers performed repetitive tasks like machines. Business leaders and stockholders saw Taylor's philosophy as a way to increase performance and profits without sharing any of the additional wealth with the workers. As a result, labor dubbed Taylor the "Enemy of the Working Man."

After a century of scientific management, organizations have come to realize that there is motivational value in sharing with the stakeholders (workers) as well as the stockholders. As we have made this transition, Fusch (1999, p. 18) wrote the following:

As the sun sets on the twentieth century
I have memories of smokestacks,
industrial expansion, assembly lines.

I remember time clocks and Fridays
and images of Taylor's scientific management
autocrats dominating human machines,
unions supporting workers in their plight.

With the dawn of a new era
I have visions of vanishing borders,
global commerce, information sharing,
and perpetual reformation.

A period of reshaping and rethinking
corporate vision and mission,
of rediscovering markets and niche
self-identity and capacity for change.

Organizational metamorphosis:
like butterflies emerging from chrysalids,
bright new ideas for empowerment,
decision-making, teamwork, and humanism.

A time of continual improvement,
shared learning, and corporate citizenship,
and from the ivory and virtual towers
of corporate universities
the birth of learning organizations.

(This material is reproduced with permission of John Wiley & Sons, Inc.)

Bowles and Gintes (1975), with their self-proclaimed radical perspectives, pointed out that most workplace performance benefits capitalists consisting of corporations and policymakers. These capitalists benefit from increased production and profits at the expense of the wage earner. They as well as numerous others have pointed out the value of recognizing workers and paying for performance—sharing the wealth. In his study of Western Manufacturing (a pseudonym), Fusch (2001a) found that the workers could see how their performance made a difference and how it led to personal rewards through 12 quarters of maximum profit sharing.

In contemporary business it is important for the organization to show a profit for its stockholders, or the company may be dissected and sold to realize a return on investment. However, for the organization's long-term health and prosperity, it is vital to share profits with stakeholders (workers), not just stockholders. As Gilbert (2007) described in his Human Competence Model, which was covered in Chapter 1, being paid for performance through profit sharing and other strategies has a direct correlation to worker behavior and willingness to perform. It is the organization's responsibility to reward people for their performance (as compared to de-rewarding—recommending and helping people decide to launch careers outside the organization). Otherwise, saving all the profits for the shareholders tends to be short-term and is the beginning of the end for many companies.

The Celestial Approach to Managing

Before geographic positioning satellites, mariners relied on the sextant and focused on the sun and other celestial bodies to navigate a course. Likewise, the Celestial Approach to Managing (see Figure 2.3) separates worker and management decisions from a specific program. It represents the freedom to focus on a task to navigate a course that leads to the desired end results. It navigates away from traditional procedures that may create barriers to realizing the desired end results, centered on the spirit of intent. The Celestial Approach to Managing therefore frees people closest to the work to make decisions, identify concepts, and affect everything a person or organization brings to a specific end result. Rather than using a two-dimensional hierarchy shown on an x-y axis, this approach metaphorically takes a more elliptical/celestial view to focus on a specific task/idea/intent that floats through the galaxy rather than a lockstep procedural hierarchy. Employing such an approach also keeps management close to the action, as discussed in the following section.

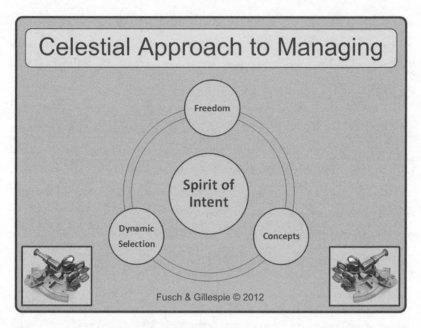

Figure 2.3 Celestial Approach to Managing

Communication and the Flow of Work

Likert (1967) used overlapping triangles in his Communication model to suggest a change in the traditional organization. It replaced the hierarchy of top-down management with one-way communication to open the flow of information up and down the organizational structure. The Work/Life Approach builds on Likert's work by suggesting that in today's global economy, organizations should take a more holistic approach toward communication and the flow of work (see Figure 2.4). For example, in the organization of today and tomorrow, communication and the flow of work need to be two-way, multi-directional communication among all workers. They must focus on the work at the closest point of action to reduce ambiguity and uncertainty in work assignments. Furthermore, our approach also represents the flow of work. People working within the organization do not need to go to the boss for decisions and assignments. Instead, people work together, and *decisions are made closest to the action.*

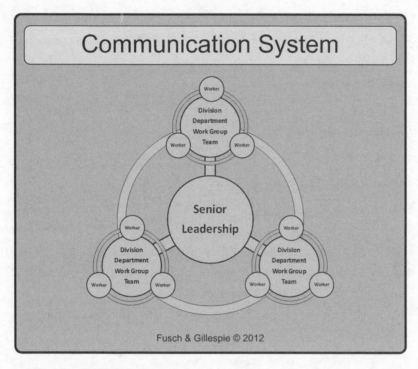

Figure 2.4 Communication system

Viewing the Communication System as a flow of work and a communication network, the flow of work begins with a customer order, production schedule, and so on. It flows through the divisions/departments/work groups/teams to the front line, where workers take the necessary actions for work completion. Moreover, the Communication System shows a flow of work and helps us identify the scope of work.

Additional Thoughts to Help You Realize Your Desired End Results

This chapter has discussed the Principles of the Work/Life Approach, the Organizational Bill of Rights, the Celestial Approach to Managing, and the Communication System. Chapter 3 looks at approaches that help us focus on the work. But first, let's explore batting averages, worker responses to telling and persuading, and focusing on the work.

Batting Averages

No one can use all the Work/Life tools all the time. We would be setting ourselves up for failure if we expected 100-percent perfection. Similar to what a good coach would say to a Little League player, just keep working on improving your batting average, and do your best. The batting average metaphor provides a positive approach to a lifelong commitment to utilize the Work/Life principles. Although we cannot use all the Work/Life approach tools all the time, we can use what works and keep using them as we strive to continuously improve our batting average.

Tell and Persuade

I'm sure you know the definitions of "I" and "you." But as Gillespie (1992) notes, it took years of working with clients for him to realize that using the word "you" when expressing a particular idea causes many people to feel as though they are being told what to do, and they react negatively. Gillespie realized that he was attempting to tell and persuade rather than asking and sharing (see Figure 2.5). When Gillespie changed his terminology to "This is my experience," the negative reactions went away.

In our youth, we were both top-notch persuaders. We got a lot done. We were unbearably intense and skilled enough to know the difference between effort and results. After introspective self-analysis, however, we realized that we could have accomplished much more with less effort if we had begun with the Work/Life Approach to using "I" when we meant "I" and "you" when we meant "you."

We have found from hundreds of business interactions that people are astounded at how much more clear the exchange of information is when there is a universal commitment to using "I" and "you" to express what is really meant. For example, sometimes people say, "You know how when you do this, such and such happens?" Our response is, "That's not true for me." This response helps people realize the power of differentiating between "I" and "you" and eliminates a possible unconscious desire to absolve personal responsibility by saying "you." This section discusses the use and misuse of "I" and "you." It also demonstrates the power of using an asking-and-sharing approach rather than a telling-and-persuading approach when working with people.

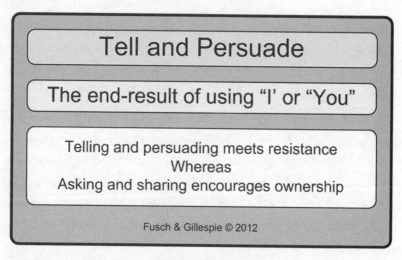

Figure 2.5 Tell and persuade versus ask and share

Telling and persuading is a long-held practice for giving direction in the "heat of battle." It often occurs when a company is overloaded with issues, short-handed, missing schedules, or running out of money or time. It also can occur because a request wasn't responded to. Perhaps the person who made the request unintentionally gave a direction that was demeaning or even mean-spirited.

It is not unusual to hear business owners and corporate executives voice frustration at being unable to get people in the business to do what they are hired to do. They complain, "To get anything done, I have to do it myself." Herein is the second mistake/limitation of successfully working toward the desired end results: Delegation carries a commitment to not doing it yourself. The first mistake is telling people what they need to do.

Another facet of "telling" is the element of "I want this"—without being clear, without recognizing the possibility that it might not be doable, without concern for the welfare of the person being told. Telling is often seen as the quickest way to get a task off someone's plate and onto someone else's, regardless of how full that other plate already is. The recipient falls into the trap of accepting the additional work. Perhaps all his or her previous efforts to reject the additional work were met with "If you can't handle it, I'll get someone else." Some put up with this type of behavior because their family has to eat. The good ones bide their time and then leave.

So how can we remember not to tell and persuade others as well as ourselves? The answer is to remember that *asking and sharing results in ownership*! There are many ways to get things done. The more latitude a person has to determine the "how to," the better the chance that he or she will complete the task beyond the stated expectations. With asking and sharing, the ownership is accepted by the people doing the work.

Indeed, telling and persuading results in resistance, whereas asking and sharing results in ownership. Telling and persuading is less effective than asking and sharing because people want to be heard. We could go on and on with hundreds of real-life examples of the limited success of companies and families because of people's powerful reaction to telling and persuading as compared to asking and sharing. Going for the win and pushing your agenda may get the job done, but ultimately it will not make you more successful. You will win the battle but lose the war. These communication tools apply both at work and at home. Although it takes time to ask and share, asking and sharing empowers people and helps you realize your desired end results.

It is pertinent to clarify direction and intentions by saying "you" when you mean "you" and "I" when you mean "I" (see Figure 2.6). As noted, saying "you" prompts resistance. However, a worker deserves clear guidance and direction when instructed on a job task. Managers should be clear that the direction is a task for the employee to perform. In addition to clarity in using "I" or "you," people need clear intentions when assigned a task. Consider the following statements from a manager to an employee:

- I think I want the Johnson proposal completed by the end of the day.
- I want the Johnson proposal completed by the end of the day.
- The Johnson proposal must be completed by the end of the day.
- I think I would like you to complete the Johnson proposal today.
- You must have the Johnson proposal completed by the end of the day.

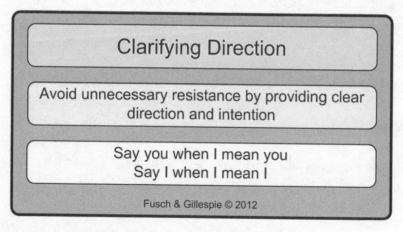

Figure 2.6 Clarifying direction

In the first three statements, it is clear that the manager wants the task completed by the end of the day; however, it is unclear who will perform the task. In the fourth statement, the manager mildly notes a desire for the employee to complete the task by the end of the day. Employees are expected to complete numerous daily tasks. Without clarity in the direction, the employee must prioritize her tasks herself and may not address the Johnson proposal. The fifth statement eliminates all ambiguity and clearly states that "You must" complete the task. In the fifth statement, the manager's direction helps the employee prioritize to complete the Johnson proposal as directed.

In summary, be careful not to misuse "you" and "I," and also clarify direction and intentions by using these two words correctly. That way, people will be freed from unnecessary resistance and ambiguity and will be able to focus on the work.

Focus on the Work

The next chapter builds on the Work/Life Approaches and the focus on the work. Knowing what our work and responsibilities are is freeing. It helps us conserve energy and be more successful. When we don't have clear roles and understand our work, we become frustrated. Furthermore, the workplace contains people from all religious, cultural, and ethnic backgrounds. Focusing on the work will enable us to work together toward desired end results.

Summary

This chapter began with the business results while considering the desired end results. This chapter has discussed the Principles of the Work/Life Approach and the Work/Life Approaches:

- The Organizational Bill of Rights and subsequent tools provide clear direction and movement for everyone working within the organization.

- The Celestial Approach to Managing frees the people closest to the work to make decisions, identify concepts, and make choices for everything a person or organization brings to a specific end result. Rather than using a two-dimensional hierarchy shown on an x-y axis, this approach takes a more elliptical/celestial view. It focuses on a specific task/idea/intent that floats through the galaxy rather than a lockstep procedural hierarchy.

- The Communication System represents the flow of work. People working within the organization do not need to go to the boss for decisions and assignments. Instead, they work together, and the decisions are made closest to the action.

- Several additional tips and strategies described how to help you realize your desired end results.

Chapter 3 focuses on the work and examines Work/Life Approaches.

3

Focusing on the Work

Being free to focus on the work allows people to be productive and excel. As noted in the preceding chapter, clarifying direction and removing resistance and ambiguity through the proper usage of "you" and "I" frees people to focus on the work. The Work/Life Approach removes uncertainty and ambiguity, clarifies direction and intention, and frees people to focus on the work. From the organizational view it is imperative to be clear on the organization's identity and purpose.

Chapter 1 discussed the critical need to integrate performance measurement, real-time strategic and operational managing, with the understanding that all businesses hope to acquire wealth in order to gain additional capital to grow and prosper. This includes the necessity of doing so *in Valuing Ways*.

Organizational Mission

Our performance improvement model (see Figure 3.1) introduced a comprehensive approach to analyzing the organization. It began with identifying the organization's vision, mission, and desired end results to identify the performance needed to support the desired end results. As we discussed, there must be a clear focus on expectations for us to focus on the work. From a "big picture" view, our Work/Life Approach for the Organizational Mission provides the first step to help us focus on the work.

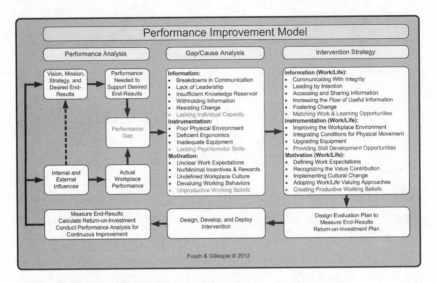

Figure 3.1 Performance improvement model

In our Work/Life Approach, we prefer a succinct organizational mission statement such as the following: "We are in business to acquire wealth so that we can gain additional capital to grow and prosper, and do so in valuing ways." To write a customized mission statement for any business in the 21st century, it is imperative to go beyond the mission of some organizations of the past (such as "Make high profits and returns for our stockholders at all costs"). It's better to take a holistic Work/Life Approach to identifying the organization's mission (see Figure 3.2).

Vision

To begin, it is important that an organization have a clear vision and that the people within the organization understand, accept, and support (UAS) the vision. (They do not have to agree with it, but they need to be heard.) There is a distinction between supporting the vision and sharing in the vision.

Figure 3.2 Organizational mission

Senge (1990) argued that when people share a commitment to a vision instead of just being compliant with a manager's vision, the organization has a shared vision. It is important to differentiate between a person committed to a vision and a person who is compliant with another's vision.

Unfortunately, it appears that Senge's ideal may be limited because management must get workers to commit to, buy into, or feel ownership of management's ideas or vision. (This ideology reflects telling and persuading, discussed in Chapter 2.)

This is apparent in the argument for aligning the workers' personal visions with the organizational vision as a whole. Following Senge's outline, some traditional corporations may employ the nomenclature to sell the workers on an organizational philosophy that essentially has not changed and likely will not lead to sustained desired end results.

We feel that because people have different personal values, ethics, and morals that influence their personal or familial vision, leadership's vision should not be forced on them.

Instead, we suggest that the people within an organization understand what the organization does and what it wants to do. They need a clear idea of the organization's vision. They also must understand how their part in supporting the vision will help the organization's mission, the stakeholders, the community, their coworkers, and themselves.

Acquiring Wealth

In addition to having a clear vision, it is vital that organizational leaders understand what it takes to acquire wealth and share it with the people in the organization. It is amazing how often we have consulted with organizations and found that leaders understand bits and pieces but don't comprehend the big picture of what it takes to acquire wealth. This was especially evident in the dot-com era. Many organizational leaders took their companies through rapid growth without a clear idea of how they were or were not acquiring wealth. When the economy shifted, many of these same leaders led their companies into insolvency.

It is also amazing how often the people working within an organization have no clue how the organization that provides their income acquires wealth. Under the Work/Life Approach, people within the organization share in the understanding of how the organization acquires wealth and works to meet the desired end results.

The Work/Life Approach also supports the notion that people relate how the organization's acquisition of wealth impacts their personal fraction of the action. Having a clear understanding of how the organization acquires wealth to gain capital to grow and prosper and how one is part of the organization frees people to focus on their work.

Stakeholders

It is vital that the organization be able to identify all stakeholders. Internal stakeholders include owners, employees, unions, and activists. External stakeholders include stockholders, vendors, partners, consumers, government (federal, state, and local), and community and civic groups.

Carroll and Buchholtz (2009) classified business stakeholders into two groups. Primary stakeholders include employees, stockholders, vendors, and partners who have a stake in the organization's success. Typically leadership must balance primary stakeholder (including internal stockholder) and employee concerns with the successful operation of the organization. Secondary stakeholders include external stockholders, consumers, government (federal, state, and local), community, environmental, and civic groups. Although they may not have a direct stake in the organization's success, secondary stakeholders do have a stake in the organization's impact on the community. Although leadership may not have the same obligations to secondary stakeholders, organizations may find that secondary stakeholders may have legitimate concerns that, if ignored, may have a negative impact on the organization's success.

Identifying stakeholders and their needs limits potential obstacles and provides business opportunities to build relationships and further realize desired end results.

Values

Chapter 6 goes into detail on the Work/Life Approach to valuing behaviors. As we conceptualize valuing behaviors as part of our Mission Statement, we should consider the organization's business ethics by asking these questions:

- What are our business ethics?
- How do we obtain understanding, acceptance, and support (UAS) for our business ethics with our stakeholders?
- What evidence/metrics do we need to show that we are adhering to our business ethics?

We like to look at the Work/Life Approach from a positive framework to build healthy organizations and productive workplaces.

In an example of an organization that did not address business ethics as a primary condition for employment, the Enron debacle at the beginning of the millennium shows how important business ethics are to an organization and all its stakeholders.

The Enron Experience

Enron Corporation was an energy-focused organization based in Houston, Texas. In 2000 Enron had 22,000 employees and was the largest electricity, natural gas, communications, and pulp and paper company in the world, with over $100 billion in revenue.

For six years *Fortune* magazine dubbed Enron America's Most Innovative Company. Wall Street marveled at Enron's continued growth and success. Then, in 2001 the world found out that Enron's innovation was in fact systematic. Creatively planned accounting fraud showed artificial growth that the company could not sustain.

In late 2001 Enron filed for bankruptcy. Its ethical violations were so egregious that the Enron name became synonymous with corporate fraud and corruption. In an effort to prevent future ethical violations, the U. S. legislature passed the Sarbanes-Oxley Act of 2002.

In addition to the employees who lost their jobs and pensions, and the public who ultimately paid for the deception, Enron's accounting partner Arthur Andersen dissolved, and company leaders went to jail.

Keeping in mind the Enron scandal and other unethical behaviors demonstrated by some organizational leaders with a "profit at any cost" mind-set, it is vital that contemporary organizational leaders demonstrate valuing behavior in the pursuit of profits and growth.

Value systems are important to a successful organization. The Work/Life Approach recognizes that sometimes people have a conflict in their personal value system with the organization's values. If that is the case, perhaps they should not work for the organization.

Growth

As organizations try to develop a mission that leads to the desired end results, it is important to address the organization's plans to grow and prosper. Well-planned growth can have a positive impact on a company. Consider the following questions when analyzing an organization's growth projections:

- What are the organization's plans to grow and prosper?
- To what extent will the growth plans lead to the desired end results?
- How will the planned growth impact the organization and its stakeholders?
- How is the organization poised to move forward with the growth plan?

As an organization looks forward to growth and prosperity, it is essential that the organization consider how its vision and mission impact all stakeholders, both internal and external. Thus emerges the notion of social responsibility.

Social Responsibility

As we embark on an era of vanishing borders and global commerce, social responsibility in today's working environment has taken on new importance. Many leading companies have long realized the value and importance of considering how business actions may impact the local community. However, in today's global economy it is important to ask this question: What is our responsibility to our community, both locally and global?

Longevity

Some organizational leaders have initiated measures to make immediate profits at the expense of the organization's future. Too often these leaders came in and helped the stock rise, collected their bonuses, and abandoned the organization, leaving others to deal with the damage. Like the Enron scandal, this is a form of unethical behavior that hurts the organization and its stakeholders.

The Work/Life Approach provides tools to make a positive impact on the organization and its stakeholders. We argue that it is important to ensure longevity in the organization versus profits in this quarter at the expense of the organization tomorrow.

The Work/Life Approach discussed in the following chapters describes several strategies to help plan for the longevity of a healthy organization.

Our People

The Work/Life Approaches covered throughout this book, such as our approach to UAS or valuing behaviors, address how to treat our people and how our people treat each other. The people make the organization.

Fusch (2001a) found in a manufacturing organization that followed the Work/Life Approach that people enjoyed going to work in the morning and felt that their company was a fun place to work. In fact, several employees had quit other positions to work for the company because they wanted to be in that working environment.

Recognizing that it is the people who make the organization, answering the following questions is critical to an organizational mission statement:

- How do we treat our employees?
- How do our people treat each other?

All too often a company's annual report to stockholders mentions how much the organization needs its people but fails to discuss any measurement metrics for them.

Mission Statement

As mentioned, a mission statement needs to describe more than just making profits. The Work/Life Approach incorporates the organization's vision, desire to acquire wealth, stakeholders, values, growth, social responsibility, plans for longevity, and people into a succinct mission statement. An example might be "We are in business to acquire wealth so that we can gain additional capital to grow and prosper, and do so in valuing ways."

Focus on the Work

Building on the mission statement to focus on the work, the Work/Life Approach starts with the idea that people know what needs to be done and are expected to do it. Managers must hold people accountable for what they were hired to do. This requires that managers follow up. If they do not want to do so, they do not belong in management.

To help focus on the work, the Work/Life Approach uses Working Guidelines. These are not rules; they are understanding, acceptance, and support (UAS) statements of behavior. When Working Guidelines are used correctly, the organization increases the flow of useful information, values people, and enhances the quality of work and work/life (see Figure 3.3).

An adage states that we deserve what we get, or we get what we deserve. Working Guidelines free people to focus on the work they are hired to do. One Working Guideline worthy of consideration specifies that you treat yourself and others with trust and respect by doing the following:

- By behaving in a caring way. (Avoid a "me first" mentality.)
- By praising positive behavior everywhere and counseling in private. Counseling in private is tough to do when emotions are running high.
- By giving and receiving feedback without blame. More will be said about this topic in Chapter 9.
- By using positive self-talk. Why would you run yourself down when others can do it better?
- By encouraging and supporting valuing behavior. After all, what's the alternative?

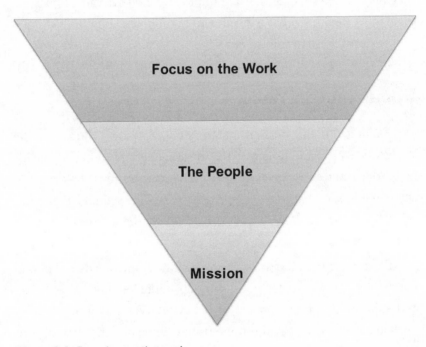

Figure 3.3 Focusing on the work

A Son's Parable

Several years ago, a father had the opportunity to give his teen-age son a tour of his workplace. During their walk through the organization's campus on a sunny afternoon, the father and son encountered the organization's president on a scenic pathway. The father introduced his son and had a short, professional conversation with the president.

As the father and son continued their tour, the son said, "I thought you didn't like him. Why were you so nice to him?"

Grasping the opportunity for a learning moment, the father explained, "Not everyone I work with will be my best friend. I don't have to like someone to work with him. However, to be successful at work, I do need to be professional and do everything possible to help my coworkers succeed. In fact, I owe it to my coworkers and my organization to put aside personal differences and do everything possible to make the workplace a successful and fun place to work."

"Oh," the son replied. "So if I get an after-school job and I don't like someone I work with, I don't have to hang out with him after work, but we need to get along and help each other at work." "Yes," said the father. "That's being a professional at work. If I were negative toward people I don't particularly like, my negativity could cause conflict that may affect my coworkers' performance as well as my own."

To continue the parable, the father further noted, "I want my company to be successful, and I want to do everything possible to help make it successful. That way, I will have better opportunities for success at work and potentially more money to go on vacations and to do the things we enjoy as a family."

The son asked, "Does this mean I should be nice to people I don't like at school too?" The father ended the discussion as they entered a building with "School is a good place to practice."

Clearly, a person does not have to like all his coworkers. However, he owes it to the organization, his coworkers, and himself to do everything possible to help them succeed. He should do the following:

- Focus on issues, situations, and tasks. Focusing on the work creates common ground for being able to deal with differences.

- Be specific. (Be clear and precise, avoiding generalities). This requires disciplined thinking.
- Tailor communications to the situation.

Another Work/Life Approach is the concept that *what I permit, I promote!* This Work/Life Approach concerns getting things done. Consider how the following affect focusing on the work:

- People often waste time at work listening to or carrying on conversations that have nothing to do with the work.
- Time, energy, and goodwill are wasted when off-color jokes, bad language, and gossip are part of a company's culture.
- Some businesses permit people to arrive late, leave early, do sloppy work, ignore safety rules, pad expense accounts, and take seemingly small office supplies.

Half of a company's mission is dedicated to creating a positive working environment by doing the following:

- Encouraging fun and enthusiasm
- Sharing rewards and success
- Being honest, fair, and productive
- Committing to achieve ever higher levels of excellence
- Promoting personal and professional growth
- Behaving in ways that value employees and express respect for everyone

When using the "What people permit, people promote" concept, the Work/Life Approach positively focuses on the work and critically influences the organization's quality of life, productivity, and profitability.

Summary

This chapter has examined the Work/Life Approach to Focusing on the Work. Building a high-performance culture and focusing on the work highlights the basic idea that the organization is dedicated to removing uncertainty and ambiguity, clarifying direction and intention, and freeing people to focus on the work.

In our examination of the Work/Life Approach to Focusing on the Work, we have reviewed the elements of an organizational mission statement and introduced Working Guidelines (that will be covered in detail later in this book) to free people to focus on the work.

Chapter 4 looks at the Work/Life Approach to sharing ideas and increasing the flow of information that is relevant, valid, timely, and reliable.

4

Increasing the Flow
of Useful Information

Sharing Ideas

In the Work/Life Approach, we look at sharing ideas that are central to the organization (see Figure 4.1). It is vital that the people who are closest to the action can share ideas. It is not unusual for a shop floor worker, custodian, receptionist, warehouse worker, or entry-level worker to come up with ideas that can have a direct impact on the desired end results for the work group and/or organization. In a workplace where people are encouraged, acknowledged, and rewarded for sharing ideas, serendipitous discoveries (unexpected outcomes) are often made, and sharing ideas becomes a valuable concept. It is unimportant who had the idea. What is important is that the idea gets used.

The Power of an Idea

As technology and knowledge expand exponentially, it is evident that ideas are powerful no matter what the source. Whether it's a new biotech discovery or an idea on how to reduce waste and save time, the power of an idea can make a considerable impact on an organization realizing the desired end results.

Gillespie (1992) noted that "People with a more narrow scope of responsibility should be encouraged to 'step ahead in time' and visualize what it looks like to have their contribution significantly increased and how it feels to be successful at doing this value added work" (p. 152).

While analyzing a growing and successful manufacturing organization, Fusch (2001a) reported that workers were encouraged to be innovative and share their ideas.

"One such innovation developed by a production worker was a clear plastic window on the side of one of the products that allowed test gauges to be observed while the unit was being tested" (p. 122). The worker's supervisor explained that the production team had been having difficulty running a quality assurance test on each product until the worker came up with the idea for a test cover with a window. Though it seemed like a simple concept, the assembly-line worker's contribution resulted in a considerable reduction in manufacturing time and overall performance improvement. This in turn had a direct impact on the desired end results for the organization.

Fusch further found that the manufacturing organization encouraged ideas throughout the organization and, more importantly, listened to people's suggestions. "In addition to workers feeling valued, during the monthly meetings, workers are recognized for their contributions" (2001a, p. 122). One of the factory workers summed up why workers shared their ideas: "employees like to be recognized" (p. 122).

Sharing ideas is the foundation for continuous organizational improvement and change. The notion of sharing ideas has two parts: People must feel safe sharing ideas, and all ideas should be considered (even if they're not implemented).

Using a traditional suggestion box may not be the best strategy. A suggestion box frequently gets ignored or increases the amount of time between conceptualization, consideration, and implementation. Moreover, the traditional suggestion box does not create a workplace in which people feel safe sharing ideas.

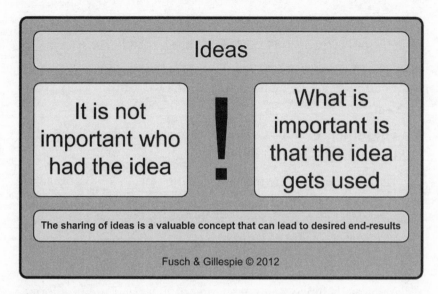

Figure 4.1 Ideas

Under the Work/Life Approach, we suggest that organizations hire people for their intellectual contributions during the course of their everyday work and give credit where credit is due. Giving people credit for their ideas helps keep them from withholding ideas because they fear the organization will not recognize them for their contributions.

Organizations spend a lot of money developing ideas, products, and services, and they are entitled to be fairly compensated for their investment and work. However, although it is important to protect intellectual property, this should not be done at the expense of losing the idea. There are ways to share ideas without abusing the source.

Useful Information

The Work/Life Approach provides methods for sharing ideas and determining what is useful information. Two extremes are related to ideas and useful information. The first extreme is withholding ideas and useful information from others who may need the information to perform better at work. This is an unacceptable behavior in any organization that can undermine the organization's success. Sharing ideas and information helps people do the work they were hired to perform.

The most prevalent form of organizational theft is the withholding of useful information.

The other extreme is too much sharing of useless information, which burdens the organization with information overload. A common example is large numbers of superfluous e-mails that are sent to everyone. Why would a worker in Chicago need to receive an e-mail stating that the coffee pot on the fourth floor in the Atlanta office is clean?

Along with supporting the sharing of ideas and useful information, the Work/Life Approach defines the characteristics of useful information.

Understanding, acceptance, and support (UAS) the characteristics of useful information should be an organizational requirement for employment. Envision the impact on time management when people quickly distinguish between needed and unneeded information. This specific Work/Life Approach directly impacts the organization's desired end results.

The Work/Life Approach provides a basic checklist to ensure that the information received is relevant, valid, timely, and reliable (see Figure 4.2). All these elements are vital to identifying useful information:

- **Relevant.** The information is pertinent to the situation.
- **Valid.** The information is accurate, understandable, meaningful, and usable, and it conveys what it is intended to express.
- **Timely.** The information is available when it is needed (not too soon, not too late).
- **Reliable.** The information comes from a trusted source (human or other).

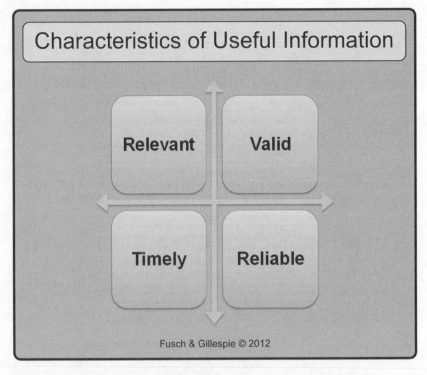

Figure 4.2 Characteristics of useful information

Levels of Information

After the useful information is processed and determined to be relevant, valid, timely, and reliable, the Work/Life Approach requires that you identify the level at which the useful information resides. The data moves from objective interpretations to more subjective interpretations, as shown in Figure 4.3.

At the most objective level of analysis, the data tends to be more real and influenced by observed reality, events, and behaviors.

Adding human perception, we include our personal feelings in the recognition of the data. We then include our beliefs in the interpretation of the information to better understand our perceptions.

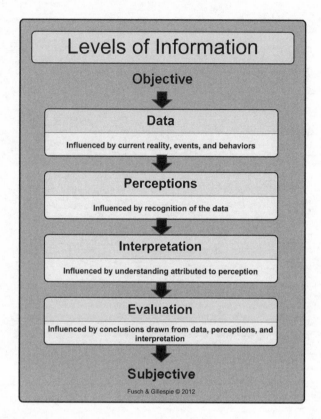

Figure 4.3 Levels of information

Finally, personal value systems help us evaluate and draw conclusions from the interpretation of the information. Although this process seems to begin with objective interpretations such as sales or performance indicators, it is the human feelings, beliefs, and values that help you analyze, clarify, and evaluate useful information.

Shelf Life of Useful Information

We've addressed the importance of having information available when it is needed. Now we'll discuss the shelf life of useful information. At the market, packaged perishables such as milk, butter, and eggs are stamped with a sell-by date. The reason for this is that at that date the product begins to spoil and may cause illness in those consuming the product. This date stamp invokes consumer trust in the product. Likewise, ideas and useful information may be valuable in helping an organization reach the desired end results when shared and used in a timely manner. However, when the idea or information is left on the shelf (out of sight, out of mind), it deteriorates and will have minimal or no value in the future. This is particularly true in high-tech industries, where an idea sitting on the shelf may see technology pass it by.

Recall the example from earlier in this chapter of the worker in the manufacturing organization. If he had left the idea of putting a window in a test housing on the shelf (in his head), the company would still be producing fewer products at a higher manufacturing cost. As soon as a useful idea is shared and implemented, people begin thinking of new ideas as a way to enhance workplace performance. When useful ideas are left on the shelf and are not used, people are less likely to continue sharing ideas.

Communicating Useful Information

When discussing useful information, particularly in the form of ideas, it is vital that the communicating person clearly communicate the idea and that the recipient correctly interpret the idea. Sometimes a manager discusses an idea that is in the early stages, looking for feedback, but the subordinate interprets the idea as a directive and acts on it. To help clarify the status of useful ideas (from wild idea to commitment) in the communication process, the Work/Life Approach uses a scale of 1 to 20 to clarify the level of thinking out loud, as shown in Figure 4.4.

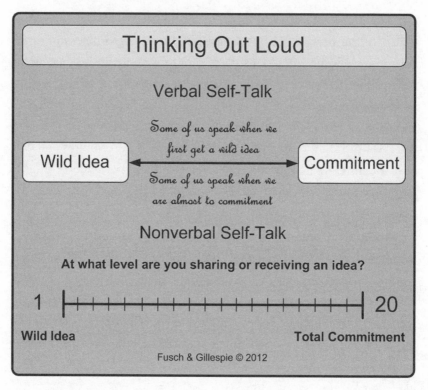

Figure 4.4 Thinking out loud

Different points on a scale may have different meanings to different people. However, the 1-to-20 scale has been an excellent approach to helping people at all levels (with different scopes of work) of the organization enhance their sharing and receiving of information and ideas. As shown in the figure, 1 is at the wild idea or brainstorming stage, and 20 is at the total commitment end of the scale. In one organization that used this scale, Fusch (2001a) found in an interview with the president that "I think that what does help unite the company is that we have a common language" (p. 102). Indeed, Fusch found that workers throughout the organization would often pull out a card and ask each other where they were on the 1-to-20 scale.

The scale did not mean that both the sharing worker and the receiving worker understood what a specific number on the scale meant to the other person. Instead, it provided a dialog and thought process for the participants in a discussion to think about how the other interpreted the idea or information being discussed.

Indeed, the 1-to-20 scale frees people regardless of their position (with different scopes of work) in the organization. The president feels free to think out loud without having to worry that someone will act prematurely. Likewise, workers throughout the organization feel free to think out loud without being criticized.

Respectful Communication

Respectful communication or listening and receiving techniques are critical in two-way communication. The recipient can completely hear the idea, and the sharing person can fully share the idea without being interrupted. The Work/Life Approach for respectful communication uses a listening-and-receiving technique. Before the recipient jumps into the conversation to discuss an idea or concept, she asks the person sharing if he is at a comma, semicolon, or period.

As shown in Figure 4.5, a comma signifies that the speaker is not done speaking. He has simply stopped to compose his thoughts and does not want to be interrupted. A semicolon also denotes that the speaker is not done speaking; however, he is willing to engage in a short dialog before continuing. If the speaker states that his idea is at a period, the recipient knows that the sharing person is done speaking and is open to hearing input and/or other discussion.

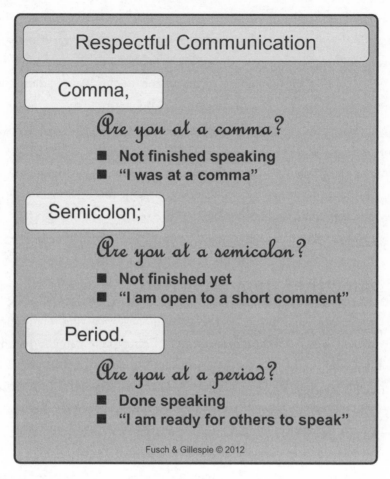

Figure 4.5 Respectful communication

Summary

In this chapter, we examined the Work/Life Approach to increasing the flow of useful information. We've discussed sharing and the power of an idea, identifying useful information and levels of useful information, thinking out loud, techniques for sharing ideas, and a respectful communication approach.

Chapter 5 looks at the Work/Life Approach to empowering others and getting people to own their "fraction of the action."

5

Getting Others to Own Their "Fraction of the Action"

In Chapter 2, we discussed the importance of understanding and clarifying what people were hired to do. Indeed, people work best when they have a clear and detailed understanding of the task they are to perform. In this chapter, we discuss the Work/Life Approach to getting others to take ownership for their jobs—owning their "fraction of the action."

In addition to people understanding what they were hired to do, the successful organization starts by hiring the right people with the right competencies to perform the job. In effect, the successful organization seeks to hire sapient workers who can help the organization realize the desired end results.

Sapiential Authority

The basic definition of *sapient* is a person who is wise and uses good judgment. The Work/Life Approach uses a model of Sapiential Authority to suggest empowering skilled people to act (see Figure 5.1). In essence, Sapiential Authority means empowering people closest to the point of action to make decisions, offer suggestions, and use their knowledge and judgment without being tied up in unnecessary bureaucratic authority.

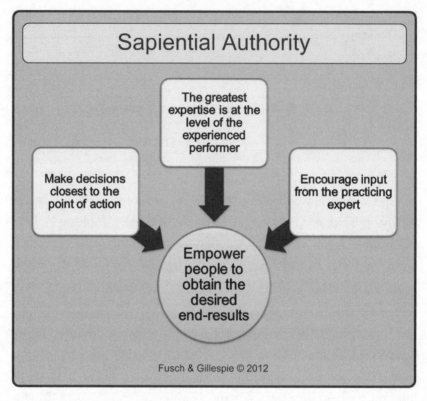

Figure 5.1 Sapiential Authority

Indeed, the Work/Life Approach using Sapiential Authority recognizes that people have the greatest expertise at the level of performance and are the best ones to make decisions closest to the point of action. This quickly resolves everyday issues, provides valuable input to leadership, and helps the organization reach the desired end results.

While observing a manufacturing facility using the Sapiential Authority Work/Life Approach, Fusch (2001a) discovered an interesting problem quickly resolved in what would often have been a major expense for many organizations.

The Case of a Quick Resolution of a Product Defect

When Fusch conducted his study at Western Manufacturing, he gave the company and its employees pseudonyms. The company embraced the Work/Life Approach and demonstrated phenomenal end results. The following is one such example of Sapiential Authority resolving a potentially costly problem closest to the point of action in minutes. This saved the company considerable rework, customer service, and money.

One demonstration of problem solving at Western Manufacturing was when worker Cris pointed out a problem with the plastic housings coming down the line. Cris told Dylan (the production lead), and Dylan asked Eric (the production supervisor) to get involved. They discussed the problem for a few minutes. Then Eric asked Padric (the production supervisor where the housings were made) to join the discussion. It appeared to the researcher that the problem had originated in Padric's division. However, all the discussions appeared professional, and no accusations were made.

The worker, lead, and supervisors worked together to find a solution to the immediate problem. They also figured out how to prevent the problem from reoccurring. All this occurred within about 30 minutes. When the researcher discussed this occurrence with Evan, the general manager (without identifying the participants or divisions), Evan philosophically shared his vision: "Visualize that [process] being routine all over the company—and most of all, they take it home and do it with their families" (2001a, pp. 121–122).

In the Western Manufacturing example, Sapiential Authority empowered people to own their contribution to the growth and development of the business. This situation occurs as a result of empowering people closest to the point of action (see Figure 5.2).

This case of a quick resolution of a product defect demonstrates the benefits of the Work/Life Approach to Sapiential Authority that empowers people closest to the point of action to realize the desired end results. However, there are too many examples of the consequences of not going to the closest point of action.

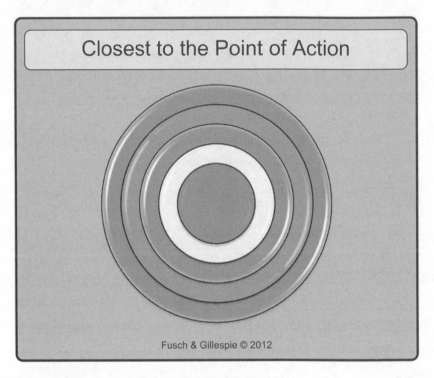

Figure 5.2 Closest to the point of action

The Consequences of Not Going to the Closest Point of Action

Fusch (2001b) analyzed a research study that demonstrated the importance of going to the people closest to the point of action. In the study, the researcher interviewed leaders from the top 100 corporate universities, including General Motors University, Motorola University, and MasterCard University. The researcher went into depth to discuss how most of these leaders came from the executive management ranks.

Given the breadth of knowledge these senior executives possess, you might think that the study findings would provide considerable insight. In the interviews, the senior leaders were asked what the organization's newly hired employees (from executive management through shop floor workers) needed in the way of knowledge, skills, and performance. The researcher discussed how it was interesting that the study findings showed that entry-level shop floor workers needed the same knowledge and skills that had traditionally been regarded as management-type skills, such as problem solving, time management, and communication.

Considering the Work/Life Approach, Fusch (2001b) argued that the study lacked validity because the senior leaders were not closest to the point of action. Had the researcher interviewed experienced shop floor workers or their supervisors at the point closest to the action, the findings may have been considerably different.

This situation occurs all too often in the world of business. Stockholders and management teams assume that people know their jobs because they currently are in those positions. People who are in a job without the knowledge, skill, and experience to do that job lack some level of competence.

We argue that it is critical to hire people with knowledge, skills, and behaviors demonstrating the ability to perform well on the job and then empower them to do their jobs. Hire the right people, and let them work. This still leaves the proposition of getting people to own their fraction of the action.

The condition of not owning the end results for being productive, profitable, and personally responsible can spread like a virus in an organization and lead to less-than-desirable end results. When brought in to help heal unhealthy organizations, Fusch and Gillespie frequently heard comments and murmurs like these:

- I was never told...
- That's not my job.
- I'm not paid to make that decision; that's management's job.
- I told them, but they don't listen to me.
- If they don't care, why should I? They make the big bucks.
- They didn't get it to me on time.
- The Board is only interested in the bottom line and the value of their stock.
- I'm only paid for eight hours. I have a life outside of this job.

Let's look at the business world from the opposite point of view. Assume that people know what they are hired to do, the results that are expected, and how they are being measured.

People throughout the organization are valued for their contribution, are paid for performance, and see themselves as stakeholders in the success of the business. This occurs as people are involved in making decisions where they are the closest point of action.

Each assignment has a scope of work that is directly under the control and influence of the person doing the work. This includes the board, the management team, and the rest of the associates. In addition, most work is done independently, dependently, and/or interdependently. To address the scope of work for each individual, it is vital to recognize that all people bring value to the organization. The Work/Life Approach points out that everyone within the organization is equal in value—just the scope of their work is different.

A key to valuing everyone no matter the scope of their work begins by respecting people. One of IBM's basic beliefs has been Respecting the Individual. This belief is a condition of employment at IBM. This belief fosters the idea for respecting others by seeking to understand what is going on when situations occur.

Understanding, Acceptance, and Support (UAS)

The Work/Life Approach uses the concept of understanding, acceptance, and support (UAS) to create an environment of shared respect leading to better workplace performance, as shown in Figure 5.3.

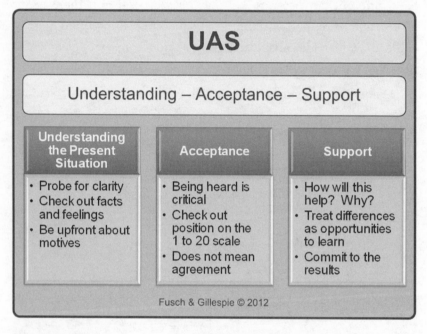

Figure 5.3 UAS

Understanding

In any conversation, understanding, acceptance, and support (UAS) begins with understanding. Understanding the present situation involves three processes: probing for clarification, checking out the facts and feelings, and being upfront about motives. When you open your mind to the concept of being clear and listening to the ideas of others, useful information (relevant, valid, timely, and reliable) is available, and you're more likely to identify the issue or idea correctly.

During the process of sharing useful information, it is important to check out the facts and feelings of the people involved. Checking to ensure that information is factual has long been standard operating procedure (SOP) in business. However, checking out how people feel about the process and information is still the exception in the business world.

A potentially negative issue occurs whenever the people involved have different perspectives that may become critical if there is not a clear understanding of the present situation. All too often, people come up with an idea about what is right and what is wrong about the issue and try to prove that their perspective is correct.

Defending individual perspectives gets in the way of sharing useful information (relevant, valid, timely, and reliable) and getting things done (see Figure 5.4).

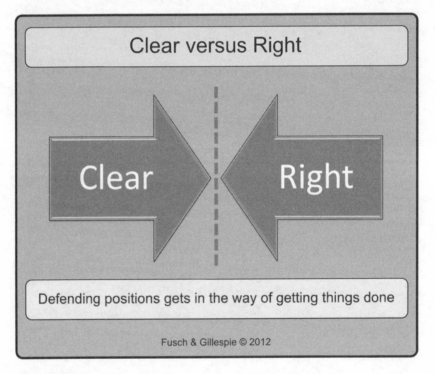

Figure 5.4 Clear versus right

In the understanding phase, people need to strive to be clear and share their perspectives. People need to seek a clear understanding of the present situation to help them reach the right decision.

Seeking to be clear instead of seeking to be right is another way to increase the flow of useful information. When dealing with issues, situations, and tasks, competent people are prepared to specifically define their view of what is happening. When they meet, each person tends to "sell" his or her position instead of seeking to be clear. Being clear provides opportunity for discussion without the competitive edge to be "right." Indeed, defending positions gets in the way of getting things done.

After clarifying and understanding the situation, it is important to check out the facts and feelings. Facts are relatively easy to verify. However, feelings are a new concept for many in relation to business discussions. For years some people have stated that there is no room for feelings in business. In years past, executives were shocked if someone asked them how they felt about a decision they had just made.

During the early development of the Work/Life Approach, one senior executive reported to Gillespie that he never ignores a feeling that raises the hair on the back of his neck. He may not act on it, but he also doesn't ignore it. Sometimes, new information later comes up that causes him to revisit that feeling. Today we argue that feelings should always be considered when discussing ideas with others to enhance UAS.

In addition to probing for clarity and checking out the facts and feelings, it is vital that we are upfront about motives (the reason why) to gain an understanding of the current situation. This means avoiding hidden agendas, sandbagging, misleading statements, and setting people up by using trick questions.

To help clarify motives, ask questions such as these: What do you want to get out of this meeting? Why are you focusing on this issue? When in doubt about motives, check them out.

Acceptance

While seeking understanding, it is important to make sure that people are being heard. Sometimes the emotional level of the issue is so strong that it overpowers the basic responsibility of staying focused on what each person is sharing. In other words, seek first to understand rather than seeking first to be understood. One of the reasons people get out of hand with their feelings is that they forget two basic conditions for getting good results:

- Failing to focus on the work and valuing work behavior.
- Being primarily focused on making sure that they are understood before understanding the position of others. This is "me-first syndrome."

As shown in the Thinking Out Loud model from Chapter 4, the scale of 1 to 20 is a key aid to acceptance. This scale frees people to stop and think about the idea or concept and provides a method for the other person to share his or her perspective.

Acceptance does not mean agreement. However, gaining acceptance requires that people be heard. Gaining acceptance also requires that people agree on behaving ethically, legally, and morally. People need to learn how to live with differences after they have been heard and a decision is made.

Support

It is not unusual for people to leave a meeting and not have their position accepted. The mistake is when they start hallway weeping and undermining the decision. This is disrespectful to everyone in the organization, is a form of insubordination, and should be grounds for dismissal. Supporting the decision, after being heard, and committing to attain the stated end results should be a condition of employment.

Here's a good question to ask yourself when you're having difficulty supporting a decision: Is this the mountain I want to die on?

A decision derived from a good UAS process often demonstrates synergy and goes a long way toward obtaining the desired end results.

Understanding, acceptance, and support (UAS) is a vital concept for gaining buy-in for decisions at the point closest to the action. However, sometimes management decides to do something without involving the people affected by that decision. A good way to include those affected by the decision using the UAS Work/Life Approach is to discuss the implementation of the decision using the following statements and questions:

- Describe what is to be done and why.
- Ask people what they like about the decision and why.
- Ask people what they don't like about it and why.
- Have people deal with what they don't like about it using the UAS concept.

The worst type of management behavior is for managers to pretend that they haven't yet made a decision, ask people for their ideas, and think people won't figure out that the decision has already been made. This type of management behavior erodes trust.

Sometimes nonmanagement people have an idea where they are at a 20 (commitment) and need to get management's buy-in. The following process is a valuable way for workers to share their ideas using the UAS Work/Life Approach:

- Describe what is to be done and why.
- Ask management what they like about the decision and why.
- Ask what they don't like about it and why.
- Ask how to gain UAS from others affected by the decision.

We believe that the Work/Life Approach to understanding, acceptance, and support (UAS) is an everyday idea that should be a part of all good business practices. People need to get in the habit of asking, "Have you UASed it?"

Arc of Distortion

As we discussed with the 1-to-20 scale, meanings are in people, not in words. The 1-to-20 scale helps people stop and discuss the meaning of what is being said so that they can better understand each other. Likewise, in UAS, the sender sends the message and ensures that the recipient understands. The recipient receives the message and ensures that he or she clearly understands the message being sent.

However, even in the best scenarios, an Arc of Distortion occurs between the message sent and the message received, as shown in Figure 5.5.

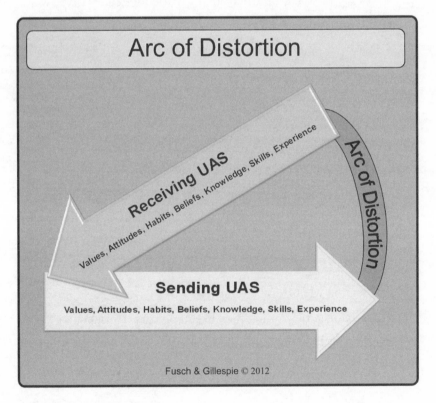

Figure 5.5 Arc of Distortion

Considering the Arc of Distortion, the sender ensures that the message sent was received correctly. The recipient ensures that the message sent was received correctly.

The Arc of Distortion occurs because people have different values, attitudes, habits, beliefs, knowledge, skills, and experience that affect how they understand the world. By adhering to the UAS Work/Life Approach, both the sender and the recipient reduce the Arc of Distortion between the sending and receiving of information. To elaborate on why the Arc of Distortion is of vital concern, consider that it's extremely unlikely that people will receive the sender's message exactly as intended. The Arc of Distortion occurs between what was sent and what was received.

The UAS concept provides a practical means to reduce the Arc of Distortion. Let's start with the idea that the sender will not convey the message perfectly. Some people are good at conveying messages, but most people are mediocre to poor. It is best to operate from the premise that everyone has room for improvement.

That being the case, the sender is obligated to seek UAS from the recipient—not because the recipient is a poor listener, but because the sender is imperfect at sending the message. The only control a sender has is being responsible for ensuring that the recipient gets the intended message.

The same condition exists for the recipient. The recipient can control only how he or she interprets the message from the sender. It is equally important for the recipient to seek UAS regarding the message sent. This is true not because the sender is poor at articulating the message, but because, from the recipient's perspective, there is no such thing as being perfect at receiving the message.

It is important that the recipient avoid comments such as "That's not what you said," "You aren't making sense," or "That's not what I heard." It can be easy for both the sender and recipient to become defensive, and everything goes downhill from there. Seeking to gain UAS from the recipient automatically reduces the Arc of Distortion.

Owning the responsibility for sending messages and owning the responsibility for receiving messages radically improves the sharing of useful information. It also improves the resolution of issues, situations, and problems. Reducing the Arc of Distortion is a vital business practice that is a condition for employment. This practice values people, ensures profitable results, increases trust, and directly helps a business grow and prosper. Meanings are in people, not in words. The notion of seeking first to understand, and then to be understood, has been around for centuries.

Summary

Getting others to own their "fraction of the action" means empowering people to take ownership of the business's problems, possibilities, growth, and prosperity. For some people this seems like a new idea, because some businesses pay outsiders to process employees through seminars to get their buy-in. And it is a tragedy when management lacks the basic competence to ensure that people have UAS about their scope of work and can't help get them involved at the point closest to the action.

People own their fraction of the action when the management team sponsors the everyday practices of gaining UAS and focusing on reducing the Arc of Distortion.

People take pride in and ownership of their jobs when they know that they are a vital part of the business, with clear responsibility, accountability, and authority. People have the freedom to act when they are responsible for their work, their needs are met, and they receive help to perform.

This chapter has examined the Work/Life Approach to getting people to own their fraction of the action. We have discussed the following:

- The importance of Sapiential Authority and empowering people to obtain the desired end results

- Sharing ideas and resolving issues closest to the point of action

- The pivotal Work/Life Approach to understanding, acceptance, and support (UAS)

- The common Arc of Distortion

- Learning to deal with being clear versus being right

As we leave this chapter, consider doing the following:

- From a manager's perspective, describe what you want to do and why. Then ask a worker these questions:
  - What do you like about the decision? Why?
  - What don't you like about it? Why?
- Then deal with what the worker doesn't like about the decision.
- From a worker's perspective, describe what you want to do and why. Then ask a manager these questions:
  - What do you like about the decision? Why?
  - What don't you like about it? Why?
  - How do I gain UAS from others affected by the decision?

In Chapter 6, we build on UAS and look at the Work/Life Approach to valuing behavior, increasing trust, and the bottom line.

6

Valuing Behavior: Increasing Trust and the Bottom Line

In Chapter 5, we introduced the Work/Life Approach that uses the concept of understanding, acceptance, and support (UAS) to create an environment of shared respect, leading to better workplace performance. In today's workplace environment, conflicts sometimes occur. In addition to showing you how to resolve conflict using UAS, this chapter provides tools that obviate some reasons for living with conflict.

Some people in business try to avoid conflict at all costs. Sometimes management turns a blind eye to people who cannot seem to get along. All too often management's answer to these types of situations is that the people involved just have a personality conflict. In other cases, when someone is being obnoxious, the manager dismisses the behavior as just that person's personality.

This concept that conflict is a personality issue is not new. In the mid- to late 20th century, personality grids became popular. Many psychiatrists and behavioral consultants encouraged management to pigeonhole people into convenient categories as a means to label them—for better or worse. This movement began when Kelly (1955) introduced his Personal Construct Theory and repertory grid as a method to understand how a person perceives and interprets his or her experience. In effect, the repertory grid and later behavioral models categorized people into groupings based on psychologically similar traits.

The movement toward categorizing people by personality and behavioral traits was an improvement over the previous lack of attention given to people in the workplace. However, categorizing people by personality and behavioral traits often became an excuse not to deal with conflict caused by poor business practices. This excuse for a lack of intervention continues to this day. People from all walks of life label people with the comment "That's just his personality." Using this excuse for inaction suggests that little can be done when someone behaves badly.

However, we argue that, in the normal course of doing business, there is no reason to label people according to personality—even in the case of personality conflicts. Many people have either heard this labeling being done or participated in doing it. We argue against labeling people who have personality conflicts because most business-people are not psychiatrists or industrial psychologists and therefore are unqualified to make that judgment.

A second point that we disagree with is that, in the normal course of doing business, people are often said to have either a good or bad attitude. The fact is, attitudes can't be seen! They are intrinsic to the human condition.

Although we cannot see attitudes, we *can* see working behavior. Under the Work/Life Approach, we look at two types of working behavior: devaluing behavior and valuing behavior. Devaluing behaviors tend to create dysfunctional tension. Dysfunctional tension causes heart attacks, loss of man-hours, strife, anger, fear, and decreased productivity due to mistakes. Here are some examples of devaluing behavior:

- Interrupting people before they finish their thought
- Ignoring people
- Not listening
- Being late for meetings

- Being disruptive in meetings
- Playing favorites
- Using anger to reflect disappointment
- Win/lose thinking
- Not sharing useful information
- Unclear work assignments
- Incomplete work assignments
- Finding fault and assigning blame
- Playing favorites
- Overpromising and underperforming
- Putdown humor
- Gossip and innuendo
- Bad language
- Not doing performance reviews
- Not paying for performance
- Discriminating because of race, creed, color, religion, age, sex, or politics
- Not having a UAS business plan
- An unclean workplace

These are just a few of the everyday devaluing behaviors that can pollute the business working environment. Devaluing behavior is caused by fear, and fear automatically breeds distrust. Fear and distrust are attitudes. Attitudes affect behavior, and behavior affects attitude. Fear and distrust are the foundation of devaluing behavior. Unfortunately, in many businesses, devaluing behavior is part of the workplace culture because leadership has not defined valuing behavior as part of the business's best practices. In fact, by not promoting valuing behaviors, the organization effectively promotes devaluing behaviors. This business practice is clearly embedded in the Work/Life concept of "What I permit, I promote."

In contrast, valuing behavior tends to eliminate dysfunctional tension and replace it with creative tension. Here are some key valuing behaviors:

- Acknowledging people for doing the right things
- Spending time seeking people's ideas for continuous improvement
- Having formal performance reviews and including opportunities for growth and development
- Setting aside time to wander around the business, sharing ideas about its strategic direction
- Ensuring that the right people are in the right jobs
- Providing opportunities for companywide events that include useful information (which is relevant, valid, timely, and reliable) regarding the business's current growth and prosperity
- Seeking people's help to focus on the work and be the best business in the marketplace

Indeed, valuing behavior is the opposite of devaluing behavior. Valuing behavior develops creative tension. Creative tension provides people with a safe working climate in which they can take informed risks, discuss differences to seek the best possible decisions, and know that they should address their mistakes to learn and grow.

Valuing Behavior

The Work/Life Approach to valuing behavior looks at the tension between devaluing and valuing behavior. Furthermore, we address how valuing behavior impacts work behavior, work attitudes, the flow of useful information, and overall performance effectiveness to accomplish the desired end results.

In Figure 6.1, the dashed line shows that valuing behavior opposes devaluing behavior. In this illustration, it is clear that devaluing behaviors lead to dysfunctional tension in work behavior. When devaluing behavior is predominant in a business, fear and distrust increase.

In contrast, when valuing behavior continues to grow, so does creative tension, which leads to increasing trust. The attitudes of generic love and trust are the foundation for a valuing working environment. *Trust automatically increases when valuing behavior increases!* The depravity of man is the main ingredient that prevents a business from operating in valuing ways!

It is also evident that devaluing behavior breeds distrust and fear and causes people to be skeptical and withhold useful information.

There are two Work/Life Approaches for increasing trust:

- Increasing valuing behavior leads to generic love and trust and causes people to be open and willing to treat each other with respect and integrity.

- Increasing the flow of *useful information* (relevant, valid, timely, and reliable) leads to increasing trust.

In practice, increasing valuing behavior (trust) and increasing the flow of useful information (trust) increases the business's overall effectiveness and increases trust in the organization.

Behavior is learned, not inherited. If devaluing behavior is the operational norm for a business, it can be replaced with valuing behavior. The question is, how willing is management (and how willing are you) to take the lead and act in valuing ways while eradicating devaluing behavior? Having learned that devaluing behavior can be replaced by focusing on valuing behavior, it is evident that change may occur regardless of age. This then challenges people in the normal workplace environment to overcome their belief that behavior is inherited.

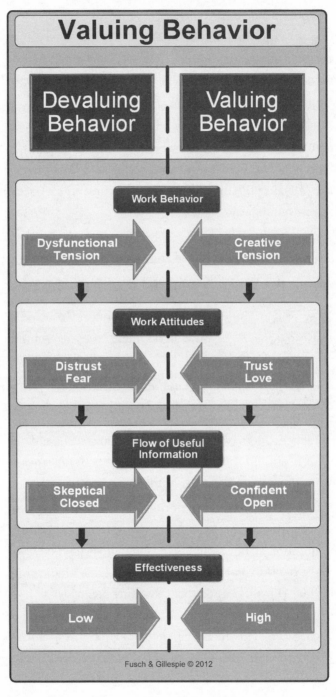

Figure 6.1 Valuing behavior versus devaluing behavior

Valuing behavior means listening to each other with the intent to understand, sharing useful information, building trust and respect. Many management people attend seminars, return to their business, and implement the fad of the day with good intentions and limited skill, resulting in the misuse of the tools. Keep in mind that actions speak so loud that people cannot hear a word you are saying. In other words, begin modeling valuing behavior. Everyone is known by their actions. From a management perspective, modeling behavior is vital for a healthy organization. Some key points for valuing behavior include the following:

- Sending a clear valuing message
- Eliminating put-down humor. Those who use put-down humor are steeped in fear and generally lack respect for others. The cumulative effects of put-down humor are lasting fear and distrust.
- Respecting people by affirming positive behavior:
  - Thank you!
  - I appreciate your work!
  - You did a great job! (describe what was good about the job)
- Listening
- Sharing useful information
- Building trust and respect
- Valuing others' perspectives

This chapter on increasing trust and ensuring continuous improvement recognizes that people spend most of their lives living in devaluing situations. Some people might feel guilty when they read this chapter, because it will remind them of their past behaviors that have hurt loved ones and coworkers. Keep in mind that this is normal. It is the changes you make after learning the Work/Life Approach to valuing behavior that will affect your future.

Stress Reduction

One challenge for people throughout the organization and in life that can also affect behavior is dealing with stress. Indeed, the medical profession has linked stress to numerous physical ailments. With the Work/Life Approach we acknowledge that behaviors, situations, and circumstances can be stressful and are often too prominent to eliminate. However, we provide methods for stress reduction (see Figure 6.2).

Figure 6.2 Stress reduction

When confronted by a stressful situation, consider the following:

- Identify the underlying issue that is causing the stress.
- Write down the cause; be honest.
- Consider what can be done about the issue.
- If nothing can be done about the issue, don't worry about it.
- Making a choice not to deal with the issue leaves the alternative, which is to keep living with the stressful situation.
- Examine the stressful situation within the sphere of influence and control.

All too often stress is beyond the individual's control. One method to help reduce a stressful situation that is beyond your control is to think of it as a matter of allocation of resources. A human brain has a limited amount of space that can be allocated to creativity, conceptual thought, work, family, faith, and dreams. Why surrender valuable brain space to a stressful issue that is beyond your control?

Many people have a lot of trouble deciding what not to do when they have too much to do, which causes them stress. The following methods can help you handle a stressful condition:

- If help is unavailable, don't worry about the situation. From a theological perspective, Martin Luther, the premier reformation theologian and founder of the Lutheran denomination, suggested that one should pray and leave the worry to God.
- Another way to look at stress is that the resulting worry is interest paid on debts not yet come due or not yet encumbered.

Much of stress is caused by conflict. Estimates show that as much as 95% of conflict is a direct result of misunderstanding. The other 5% of conflict is most likely a result of a mismatch between beliefs and values. **Understanding, acceptance, and support** (UAS) and the Arc of Distortion are Work/Life Approaches designed to minimize misunderstandings. To state the obvious, the Work/Life Approaches must be used to be of any value.

Indeed, stress reduction can help you work and live happier as well as better model valuing behaviors. The way we feel about situations and behaviors is legitimate, and we must be responsible for our actions.

Building on the Work/Life Approach for valuing behavior, considering that feelings are legitimate and that people perceive situations differently, validating people for their contributions to the organization can lead to UAS and increasing trust to affect the bottom line.

Validations

Sometimes you can improve your personal or working relationships by taking time to seek out opportunities to give positive feedback. Sometimes this is called giving a compliment. The Work/Life Approach equivalent to a compliment is called a validation. The reason for the difference in terms is that compliments have a history of being used to flatter, impress, and gain favor from others. Many people have had bad experiences with both receiving and giving compliments. People want positive feedback when it is due. The following reflects the Work/Life Approach for giving and receiving validations.

Giving and receiving sincere validations can be powerful in the workplace and can make a positive difference in people's lives. Since Gillespie (1992) first introduced the concept of giving and receiving validations in the workplace, it is amazing the impact that this Work/Life Approach has made. In his study at Western Manufacturing, Fusch (2001a) found that giving and receiving validations produced a powerful emotional bond between the company's workers. Furthermore, validations augmented Understanding, Acceptance, and Support (UAS) and modeling behavior that helped create an environment of shared respect and a place where people wanted to go every day.

Validations are something positive that people see, feel, know, believe, and share about a person or group. This process is a way to value people and share useful information (relevant, valid, timely, and reliable). The ultimate end result is increasing trust.

As Fusch (2001a) noted, giving and receiving validations at first may feel awkward. However, sincere and genuine validations impact people's feelings and their performance in the workplace. The Work/Life Approach to giving validations specifies that you should do the following (see Figure 6.3):

- Be clear and specific about the validation, relating it to a valuing behavior. Just saying "You did a good job" is of little value. Describe what was good about the job.

- Talk directly to the person deserving validation. Consider the potential impact when people hear about another's perceptions only secondhand.

- Make validations sincere and genuine. People are smart; they know if a validation is sincere. Insincere validations are deceitful and are akin to putting fresh frosting on a stale cake.

- Make sure that no strings are attached to validations. Hidden motives are dishonest.

- Be aware of the person's feelings when giving validations. This is important when people are new to receiving validations, because they may feel somewhat awkward. Feelings are legitimate, so actions must be responsible.

- Be open to giving validations in public around others and one-on-one in private.

- Seek opportunities to give more validations.

- Help others become familiar with these elements, and practice giving validations so that they become part of the fiber of the business.

- When giving a validation to someone who tries to brush it off, recognize that hearing a validation may be new to that person. Let him know that the validation is a gift he deserves.

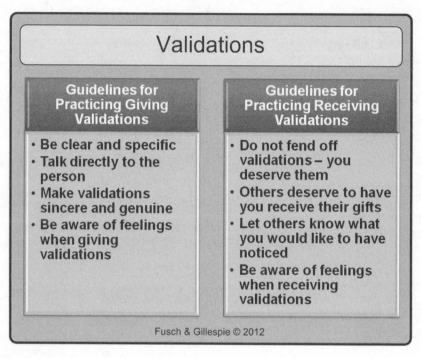

Figure 6.3 Validations

The Work/Life Approach to receiving validations specifies that you should do the following:

- Recognize that you deserve the validation. Avoid the temptation to shrug off a validation given in good faith. The person giving it could be hurt by your dismissal of her sincerity.

- People usually want validations. However, be aware of whether you send signals that seem to indicate that you don't want validations. You might end up not receiving the validations you deserve.

- Graciously receiving a validation is the same as receiving a gift. People deserve to have their gifts received and appreciated.

- Listening carefully to a validation shows respect for the person giving it. Respect for that individual automatically increases trust.

- Share with others your behaviors and accomplishments that you would like them to notice.

- Tell the person how the validation makes you feel. Sometimes in a business setting, people are given a validation for the first time in 20 years. Some people have never received one.

To act or not is each person's prerogative. Aim for a life of valuing behavior, trust, and continuous sharing of useful information. As we give and receive validations, as we strive to reduce stress, and as we endeavor to demonstrate valuing behaviors, it is clear that we can project a behavior toward others. The Work/Life Approach provides a Whole Person Model that addresses how people adjust their attributes as needed for individual situations.

The Whole Person Model

The Whole Person Model, shown in Figure 6.4, recognizes that people have feelings, thoughts, and physical attributes. These change during the workday and need to be considered when you respond to different situations. In a nutshell, feelings affect subjective and intangible attributes. Thoughts affect objective and tangible attributes. Physical attributes require food, rest, recreation, and hygiene. How people perceive these attributes and behavior affects how they respond and interact in the workplace.

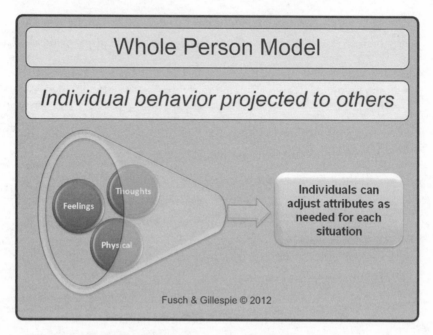

Figure 6.4 Whole Person Model

When reflecting on the methods to reduce workplace conflict, enhancing valuing behavior, and giving validations, remember that the Work/Life Approach was designed to help companies stay focused on their core values. Doing so will help them develop a healthy and productive working environment that drives them toward their desired end results.

Summary

In this chapter, we examined the Work/Life Approach to valuing behavior, reducing stress, and giving and receiving validations. It explored what influences our behavior and looked at increasing trust that impacts the bottom line.

Although all these Work/Life Approaches are important, the central issues in this chapter focus on the following questions:

- How willing is management (and how willing are you) to take the lead and act in valuing ways while eradicating devaluing behavior?

- How willing is management (and how willing are you) to take the lead in giving and receiving validations?

- How will you address stress? What methods will you use to reduce stress and worry?

In Chapter 7, we explore the Work/Life Approach to owning the present condition. This helps define the future condition and emphasizes the need to do what's right because it's right—even when it doesn't feel right.

7

Owning the Present Condition Helps Define the Future Condition

An old adage says that there is *never time to do it right and always time to do it over*. Sometimes people rush to complete a project by doing less-than-adequate work with the idea that they can make corrections later. However, there may not be enough time to do so. Analyzing the adage, we can argue that it is far better to spend time doing the task right the first time and then move on to the next project. If you perform tasks well the first time, without any need for rework, the more time you have to pursue future projects. In other words, owning the present condition helps define the future condition.

In this chapter, we refute the old adage. Owning the present condition helps define the future condition and emphasizes the need to do what's right because it's right—even when it doesn't feel right. When the present condition fosters the continuous flow of useful information, technically and behaviorally during the press of everyday business, people are part of creating what the *desired future condition looks like*. The challenge that many organizations face is linking the strategic direction for the desired future condition to the actual day-to-day operations. Indeed, owning the present condition helps define the future condition.

The Work/Life Approach provides a Managing System methodology to help demonstrate the process of developing a workplace that addresses the impact of the organization's vision and strategic direction on the present and future work. The Work/Life Approach to managing bridges the gap between the strategic arena and operational arena.

Managing System Overview

The Work/Life Approach provides a Managing System that is an iterative process linking the different attributes of the strategic arena to the operational arena. All too often organizational leaders are either good strategists or good operational managers. However, seldom do leaders look at the Managing System as an iterative cycle that takes the strategic spirit of intent to the day-to-day operations. As we noted earlier in this book, sometimes organizations bring in or send managers to dynamic workshops and presentations, but the participants return lacking the link between the intentions and practical application. Throughout this book we have introduced powerful Work/Life Approaches that provide practical (how-to) strategies to implement in daily operations. The following sections explain the Work/Life Approach to the Managing System.

Strategic Arena

Beginning with the spirit of good intentions, the strategic arena encompasses five key areas that impact performance and help you realize the desired end results: planning, organizing, directing, leading, and controlling (see Figure 7.1).

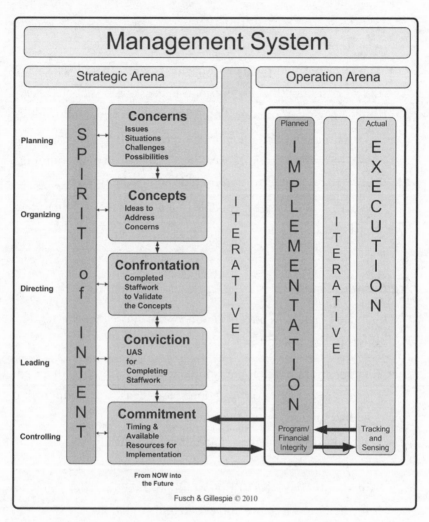

Figure 7.1 Management System

Planning

Planning includes concerns such as issues, situations, challenges, and possibilities. Planning by definition is looking to the future to decide what to do today. (The future may be an hour, week, months, or years from now.) The Work/Life Approach to aid in planning includes the following:

- The Organizational Bill of Rights ensures that people can do what they were hired to do.

- The Celestial Approach to Managing frees the people closest to the work to identify concepts and make decisions about everything a person or organization brings to a specific end result.

- A clear mission statement might say something such as "We are in business to acquire wealth so that we can gain additional capital to grow and prosper, and do so in valuing ways."

- Working Guidelines free people to focus on the work they were hired to do.

Organizing

Organizing includes concepts and ideas to address concerns. The Work/Life Approach includes the following:

- Ideas central to the organization are shared. It is vital that people who are closest to the action share ideas. It is unimportant who had the idea—just that the idea gets used.

- Methods for sharing ideas and determining useful information: relevant, valid, timely, and reliable.

- You identify the level of the useful information from objective interpretations to more subjective interpretations.

- You ensure that the right people are in place to do the work.

Directing

Directing includes confrontation leading to completed staff work to validate concepts. The Work/Life Approach to directing includes the following:

- A model of Sapiential Authority suggests empowering skilled people to act. In essence, Sapiential Authority means empowering the people who are closest to the point of action to make decisions, make suggestions, and use their knowledge and judgment without being tied up in bureaucracy.

- The Organizational Bill of Rights and Working Guidelines provide understanding and clarification of what people were hired to do. This includes providing the necessary level of direction based on the person's knowledge, skills, and experience.
- Use communication techniques such as asking the person sharing if she is at a comma, semicolon, or period; using the 1-to-20 scale; and using "I" when you mean "I" and "you" when you mean "you."
- Understanding, acceptance, and support (UAS) and giving validations.

Leading

Leading includes understanding, acceptance, and support (UAS) for completing staff work and giving validations. Moreover, leading provides vision, hope, excitement, and energy for inspiring people. The Work/Life Approach to leading also includes methods that will be discussed in later chapters, such as managing by walking around (MBWA).

Controlling

Controlling includes commitment to the Work/Life Approach discussed in this book and adherence to the Organizational Bill of Rights to provide timing and available resources for implementation. Controlling also includes internal policies, practices, and procedures, as well as requirements necessary to address external legal, financial, moral, and ethical regulations.

Iterative

The Work/Life Approach to the Managing System is an iterative process linking the different attributes of the strategic arena to the operational arena. The Managing System is an iterative cycle that takes the strategic spirit of intent to the day-to-day operations. The iterative process moves from a traditional linear strategy to a holistic cycle that repetitively and continuously links the strategic and operational arenas as needed.

Likewise, within the operational arena, the iterative process provides a repetitive and continuous link between the planned implementation of a project/operation and the actual execution of the project/operation as needed.

The iterative process leads to the desired end results; however, the iterative process does not have a defined endpoint. Instead, the iterative process is continual, free-flowing, and continuously changing. Issues arise and interactions occur from new information as well as internal and external influences such as people within the organization, customers, vendors, competitors, and stakeholders.

Operational Arena

The operational arena uses Work/Life Approaches to link the planned implementation to the actual execution. Furthermore, the operational arena iteratively links program financial integrity to tracking and sensing such as performance indicators, cost, and return on investment. Likewise, the operational arena uses Work/Life Approaches to iteratively link the actual spirit of intent through strategic planning, organizing, directing, leading, and controlling with the execution of the work.

Using the Work/Life Approach to the Managing System, organizations can span the traditional divide between strategic managing and operational managing, which is the execution of the work. This is a considerable leap from the metaphorically viewed isolated towers of strategic management and operations management. Viewed from an iterative process, organizations can concentrate on performance and quality to realize desired end results.

Quality Management

In essence, quality is one of the most debated words in organizations today. Most dictionaries define *quality* as a noun that describes what an element contains or the degree of excellence attributed to a commodity. Fusch notes one observation in which the board of directors for an institution of higher education spent close to a year of board meetings debating a revision for the mission statement. After the long debates, the revised mission statement added the adjective "high," which changed the mission from providing quality education to providing high-quality education.

As a result of the United States Malcolm Baldrige National Quality Improvement Act of 1987, the National Institute of Standards and Technology (NIST) manages the Malcolm Baldrige Quality Award for Performance Excellence. NIST (2011, paragraph 2) defines quality in performance excellence as an integrated approach to organizational performance management that results in the following:

- Delivery of ever-improving value to customers and stakeholders, contributing to organizational sustainability
- Improvement in overall organizational effectiveness and capabilities
- Organizational and personal learning

Whether you agree with NIST's holistic definition for performance excellence or choose to use adjectives such as high, top, stellar, or excellent, we argue that it is important to view quality as a continuous process. There is an important distinction between the linear definition of what an element contains and a continuous process that strives for improvement. All too often organizations stop when a level of quality is met, only to be passed by competitors, resulting in a loss of market share.

The Impact of Quality on the Automotive Marketplace

Near the end of the 20th century, American automakers adhered to a traditional quality control methodology and did not address customer satisfaction and performance improvement. This led to offshore competitors surpassing American automakers in quality and a substantial loss in market share. Awareness of global competition came about in the 1980s, after Japanese automobile manufacturers successfully increased their percentage of sales in the U.S. market.

In response to the new global competition, Western enterprises explored ways to restructure and strengthen their organizations by implementing certain Japanese models. These included operator responsibility for quality, continuous improvement, quality circles, statistical process control, design for manufacture, setup time reductions, just-in-time production, total quality control, cellular manufacture, and kanban materials control (Nonaka & Takeuchi, 1995).

It was evident that American automakers learned about quality the hard way as they watched their market share dwindle and offshore competitors gain strong market share. In contrast to the traditional linear perspective of stopping when a standard is met, the Work/Life Approach to Quality Management is a holistic and continuous process.

As shown in Figure 7.2, the Work/Life Approach to Quality Management views the process as continuous quality analysis, quality planning, quality controls, quality assurance, and quality improvement. In addition to viewing quality management as a continuous process, the

Work/Life Approach uses Sapiential Authority to suggest empowering skilled people closest to the point of action to make quality decisions, make suggestions, and use their knowledge and judgment without being tied up in bureaucracy.

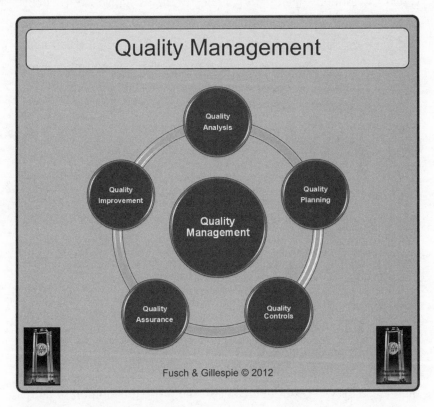

Figure 7.2 Quality Management

When tasks are performed and commodities built embracing sapiential authority for Quality Management while striving for continuous improvement, quality will be a continuous process, and the present condition helps define the future condition. Another present condition that helps define the future condition is the reduction of mosaic threat assessments.

Mosaic

The Work/Life Approach defines a mosaic as a cumulative picture of an organization's spirit of intent for success. Originally, mosaic threat assessments dealt with violence in the workplace and schools, as well as methods for law enforcement to assess and screen threats and inappropriate communications. In the organization, risk managers look at the threat score: threat = probability × seriousness. From a risk perspective, we suggest that it is important to understand what it takes to meet demands in business and how negative issues can impact the desired end result.

It is important to remember that no one knows what is going on all the time. Therefore, when seeking to understand where the business is now, it is equally important to recognize that people's cumulative knowledge is like a mosaic. Increasing trust makes it possible for synergy to occur. (Synergy is where 1 + 1 = 3 or more.) When we follow this process, we are managing for synergy.

From the Work/Life Approach, we view the mosaic as removing the negatives to reach the desired condition (see Figure 7.3). As depicted in the mosaic model, real positive and real negative issues expend opposing energy. If we can reduce the negative issues and move from the current situation, we can realize synergy, and trust will increase. This will result in change to the present condition to define the future condition.

Four key elements provide a comprehensive mosaic of the situation and can help you move from the present condition to the desired future condition:

- **Communicating how what is happening affects you.** This relates to the Work/Life concept of conditions for success. This means that sometimes people need help from others to complete their work and must have understanding, acceptance, and support (UAS) from others to complete their work successfully.

- **Explaining what you need from others.** If others do not exhibit UAS about what is needed, the desired end results will not be met.

- **Understanding what the situation means to you.** It wastes time when situations move beyond people's chance to reach UAS on a situation. Each person is responsible for slowing down the process and reaching UAS.

- **Defining conditions for success.** Sometimes you need help from others, and you need resources that are not under the control and/or influence of the person responsible for getting the job done.

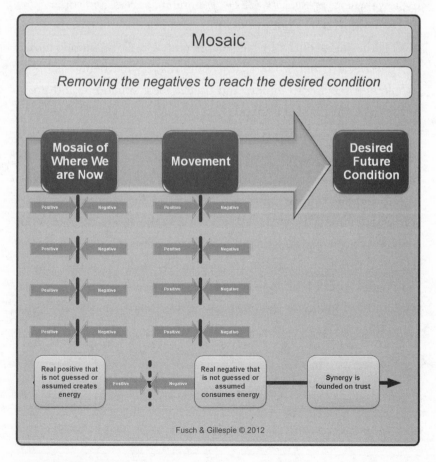

Figure 7.3 Mosaic

To eliminate negatives, people can suspend disbelief and envision success for themselves and others. Everyone makes mistakes. It is what is done after a mistake is made that fosters openness and trust. Suspending disbelief gives the person the benefit of the doubt with the understanding that the mistake wasn't intentional. Envisioning the person's future success reflects confidence in that person and increases trust. Have fun, and encourage others to do the same. Remember the proverbial phrase that you can attract more flies with honey than with vinegar.

From a threat perspective, there is a common misperception in the business world that management knows what is going on. In reality, few owners, presidents, CFOs, general managers, and supervisors make an effort to get out of the office and wander through the business, gathering a sense of what's happening. From the mosaic model perspective, it is important that leaders realize that being visible to people and seeking to understand their issues, situations, and problems create trust and confidence.

Although not exclusive to the Work/Life Approach, MBWA is a valuable process for gathering useful information. In fact, MBWA has been around since John Henry Patterson of National Cash Register introduced the concept in the late 1800s. His sales manager, T.J. Watson, who founded IBM, carried MBWA into the 1900s. MBWA is not intended to catch people doing things wrong. It is intended to inspire and reflect personal interest. It also validates the idea that resolving negatives and building on positives is a healthy way to increase trust and confidence as the business moves toward the desired future condition.

Summary

In this chapter, we examined the Work/Life Approach to owning the present condition to help define the future condition. In particular, this chapter covered the following topics:

- The Managing System bridges the gap between the strategic arena and the operational arena.
- Quality management is a holistic and continuous process.
- The mosaic removes negatives and builds on positives to increase trust and help you reach the desired condition.

We also have shown how the Work/Life Approach to the Managing System incorporates the methods we have analyzed throughout this book. Relevant, valid, timely, and reliable information defines useful information that, when shared, automatically increases trust. It's important to increase trust throughout the organization.

In Chapter 8, we explore the Work/Life Approach to problem solving.

8

Fifty Years of Problem Solving: A Magnificent Obsession

The title of this chapter indicates that the authors bring substantial experience to problem solving. However, the details of the authors' experience are beyond the scope of this chapter, leaving the focus on the Work/Life Approach to problem solving. In 1906, Italian economist Vilfredo Pareto observed the distribution of income and wealth and introduced what he called the 80/20 rule in which 80 percent of the wealth was controlled by 20 percent of the people and that 20 percent of the people controlled 80 percent of the wealth. Later, Joseph M. Juran dubbed Pareto's 80/20 rule as the Pareto Principle of mal-distribution and argued that 20 percent of people' effort (*the vital few*) produced 80 percent of the results and 80 percent of people's efforts (*the trivial many*) produced 20 percent of the results (Edmund & Juran, 2008).

The 80/20 Rule / Pareto Principle

- 20 percent of the people control 80 percent of the wealth.
- 80 percent of the people control 20 percent of the wealth.
- 20 percent of the effort produces 80 percent of the results.
- 80 percent of the effort produces 20 percent of the results.

From a management perspective, it is important to focus on the *vital few*. It's equally important to deal with the *trivial many*. This means being clear about the value of each person's contribution before making a reduction in force.

In addition to the vital few and the trivial many, you need to also consider the *trivial mandatory*. The trivial mandatory is work that has to be accomplished for the business' primary work to get done. This could be heating the building, safety, maintenance, payroll, facility upkeep, and so on. There are responsibilities to complete work that are the trivial mandatory and without this effort, the organization would suffer.

However, the 80/20 rule also suggests that 20 percent of the effort produces 80 percent of the results (the vital few) and that 80 percent of the effort produces 20 percent of the results (the trivial many). From a management perspective, it is important not to make the *trivial many* the *trivial mandatory*. One of the quickest ways to change this rule and improve performance is through prioritizing and time management.

Prioritizing and Time Management

The Work/Life Approach to prioritizing and time management is a simple yet powerful process.

Consider a matrix with three columns and three rows, as shown in Figure 8.1. From left to right, the columns indicate tasks over which you have almost complete influence and control, tasks over which you have considerable influence and some control, and tasks over which you have very little influence and almost no control. It is clear that you can make the biggest impact with tasks over which you have almost complete influence and control. In contrast, with the tasks over which you have little influence and control, tasks may go uncompleted, and you may not make much of an impact. Therefore, it stands to reason that most of your efforts should be dedicated to the first and second columns.

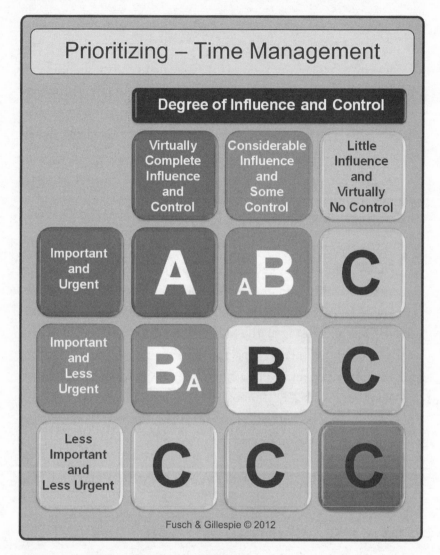

Figure 8.1 Prioritizing and time management

Similar to the columns, the rows from top to bottom indicate tasks that are important and urgent, tasks that are important but less urgent, and tasks that are less important and less urgent. This suggests that you should address the important and urgent tasks first. Then, if time allows, you should address the tasks that are important and less urgent. Unless you have considerable extra time, you should decide whether you even need to consider working on tasks that are less important and less urgent.

Viewing the matrix, it is clear that your first priority should be to complete tasks in the A category. You have almost complete influence and control over these tasks, and they are important and urgent. This category will make the biggest impact on your productivity and should be your first priority.

AB and BA should be given second priority. The AB category indicates important and urgent tasks over which you have considerable influence and control. The BA category indicates important but less urgent tasks over which you have complete influence and control.

When you have completed all your first- and second-priority tasks, you should identify any first- or second-priority tasks that you can perform to help your coworkers and improve organizational performance. After addressing all the tasks that have first- and second-level priority, you should address tasks in the B category. You have considerable influence and some control over these tasks, and they are important but less urgent. In most cases, you should consider tasks in the C category nonessential. They should be addressed only during less-busy times—or even eliminated.

> ### Caution
>
> Before you consider eliminating a job task, analyze how doing so will impact the work of others' work. A task that is unimportant in one area may be very important in another area.

People often do not properly prioritize their tasks, which leads to time-management challenges. Although during a given workday priorities may change, failure to prioritize tasks may lead to wasting valuable time and resources jumping from one crisis to another. The following sidebar describes how Joe Smith, Jim Anderson, and Jane Doe handle time-management challenges.

Time Management Challenges

Joe Smith

Joe is one of the hardest workers at Western Manufacturing. He comes in early each day, takes few breaks, and strives to get all his work done. Joe always prioritizes his work by what is most urgent and completes most of the important and urgent work in categories A, BA, and C.

Even though Joe has little control over the important and urgent work in category C, he ends up spending over half of his time on these tasks. The large amount of time Joe must spend on work that he has little control over prevents him from addressing work in the important and less-urgent categories. Left undone, work in the BA category soon moves into the A category, and Joe frequently finds himself in a state of crisis management.

Jim Anderson

Jim prides himself on being a smart worker. He addresses tasks that he has almost complete influence and control over, including A, BA, and C. He feels that this makes his job easier. Because he completes many tasks, he believes he is a top performer.

Unfortunately, Jim's work on the easy tasks in category C that are less important and less urgent takes up the time he could be using to address important and urgent tasks in category AB. From an organizational perspective, Jim is not a top performer and does not prioritize to help the organization realize its desired end results.

Furthermore, frequently tasks in the AB category reach the crisis stage. Jim lets the organization down when others have to pick up his AB tasks.

Jane Doe

Throughout each day, Jane quickly assesses and reassesses her priorities. First she addresses tasks in the A category, followed by tasks in the BA and AB categories. Managers and coworkers at Western Manufacturing view Jane as an efficient team member who can be counted on to get the job done and help the organization realize its desired end results.

Joe, Jim, and Jane all do some prioritizing. However, it is clear that Jane's method of adhering to the Work/Life Approach for prioritizing and time management makes her a more productive worker. Consider what happens when people do not prioritize—crisis management may be needed.

Numerous books are available on time management, and time management consultants make a good living showing people how to be more effective. In most cases, using the Work/Life Approach to prioritizing and time management, supplemented by thinking about the consequences that will result from performing the task, improve workplace performance. For example, many people open their mail and, due to lack of time, quickly scan, sort, and place the items in a stack to review when they have more time. For the benefit of this example, we will refer to a specific piece of mail as the *blue pamphlet*. After a few months the blue pamphlet is in a large stack and has been handled dozens of times, reviewed, and resorted in the pile. Finally, after the stack of mail gets too high, you decide to toss the blue pamphlet in the trash.

Consider how much time you wasted reviewing and sorting the stack each day, only to eventually throw away the blue pamphlet. In some workplaces we have observed people spending as much as an hour a day opening mail, checking their in-box, perusing, and sorting. A more conservative estimate is that many people spend 30 minutes on such tasks each day. This equals 125 hours per year. Considering the number of years the average person works, this equates to almost 2.7 years of your career spent on just perusing and sorting blue pamphlets that will eventually end up in the trash.

Consider the following technique. When opening mail or clearing your in-box, stand over the trash can. Standing is often less comfortable than sitting and therefore helps you get through a task faster. Quickly look at each item (blue pamphlet) and do the following:

- If the blue pamphlet is nonessential, drop it in the trash.
- If it looks like it may be interesting to read when you have more time, drop it in the trash.
- If it is useful information that others need, pass it on.
- If it is useful information that needs to be addressed or filed, address the information or file it. Do not leave it for later.

Using this method, you handle the blue pamphlet only once. You can quickly take care of all the blue pamphlets and save considerable time that then can be allocated to tasks with high priorities. Likewise, with e-mail, a good strategy is to either delete, forward, or address it quickly to avoid wasting time sorting and reading it repeatedly.

Although the Work/Life Approach to prioritizing and time management is a simple yet powerful process, people often don't prioritize. In essence, failing to prioritize is subscribing to the philosophy that there is never enough time to do it right and plenty of time to do it over. The Work/Life Approach to prioritizing and time management prevents problems from occurring and has a positive impact on problem solving. Remember the adage that an ounce of prevention is worth a pound of cure.

The Basics of Solving Problems and Making Decisions

One of the key ways to get things done is to know how to solve problems and make decisions. Before we go into the specifics of how to do so, here are some basic practices to consider:

- Avoid the "hurry up and wait" phenomenon. When things are not going well, people tend to metaphorically grab for the first straw that looks promising, spin their wheels, and run out of gas.

- Avoid organizational pollution by eliminating untouchable policies, practices, and procedures:
  - We can't consider that because...
  - That's someone else's responsibility.
  - They don't want to hear about problems, only solutions.
  - I need to run that by...
  - Remember what happened the last time we tried that?
  - You don't have to live with it like I do.
- Have a sense of urgency that matches the understanding, acceptance, and support (UAS) schedule of work—not too soon, and not too late.
- Recognize when time is of the essence. Time has a limiting qualification starting with "It depends...". This phrase is an excuse to avoid continuing to deal with the problem in the present.
- Ask open-ended questions that lead to gathering more useful information. What, where, when, how, and why questions offer opportunities to explore a number of diverse directions.
- Avoid asking yes-or-no questions; they tend to stop the flow of additional useful information. However, sometimes yes-or-no questions are appropriate. In these instances, following them with a "why" question helps reopen the dialog.
- Constantly seek facts and feelings as interdependent elements.
- Follow the UAS concept throughout the whole problem-solving and decision-making process.
- Be open to "thinking out loud" and using the Working Guidelines to facilitate the flow of useful information (relevant, valid, timely, and reliable).
- Avoid premature closure—making decisions with insufficient information and limited understanding.
- Focus on the work to be done and work behavior that values the people involved in the process.

Very few businesses have specific company problem-solving and decision-making processes. This means that some of the most vital work is left up to "experiential learning" and often yields incomplete staff work, wasted time doing rework, and unnecessary cost.

It is unbelievable that with our current technological information systems, people ignore their obligation to ensure that specific knowledge, skills, and experience (competence) are necessary to be proficient at problem solving and decision making.

Problem Solving: Analyzing the Situation, Expectations, and Actions

Problem solving starts with concern about a particular situation. There are usually plenty of opportunities (and not enough time) to work on a situation that *seems* to be a problem. A situation is often a condition that *seems* to be getting in the way of accomplishing the vital work necessary to produce products and/or services for customers. The key phrase here is that *it seems to be getting in the way*. This indicates that you're unsure *what's happening* or *what's going on*.

The Work/Life Approach uses the situation, expectations, and actions (SEA) model for problem solving. It provides a succinct and clear method to go beyond the surface and focus on the underlying issues. Using understanding, acceptance, and support (UAS) to begin the problem-solving process, you can follow these steps to clarify the situation (see Figure 8.2):

- Through UAS, identify what is occurring.
- Through UAS, identify what should be occurring.
- Through UAS, identify the differences between or deviations from what is occurring versus what should be occurring; these differences can be a problem.

- Through UAS, identify the causes of the differences or deviations.

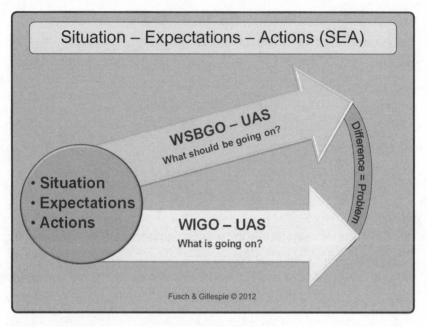

Figure 8.2 Situation, expectations, and actions

Finding the root cause is important. The most obvious cause may not be the root cause. Many times there are primary, secondary, and tertiary causes. This means that seeking the root cause becomes an iterative process. We seek the root cause by asking why as many as five times before the root cause may be discovered. In other words, when asking why something is causing a gap between what should be going on (WSBGO) versus what is going on (WIGO), you should ask why again as many times as necessary to help uncover the problem's root cause. A situation is not a problem until you identify a gap between WSBGO and WIGO. If or when differences and deviations no longer exist, there is no problem, and no further attention is needed.

Sometimes outside expertise is sought to get to the root cause. Metaphorically, this is due to the organizational blinders that people frequently have when they are too close to the issues. The discipline for following the SEA sequence ensures that the next step (decision making) will yield resolution of the problem.

Decision Making

A decision is in effect a choice of alternatives. Alternatives are the means for resolving the cause or causes of the differences or deviations. Sometimes people want to jump directly from differences and/or deviations to developing alternatives without determining the cause, let alone the root cause.

There are also times when *what is required* may not be the best for the business at the time. It could be that the tolerances on a part no longer fit, that previous target dates no longer are realistic, or that budget assumptions or customer requirements have changed.

It is important that UAS exists for the changes in what should be going on (WSBGO) and/or that there is no change in WSBGO. If WSBGO is still accurate, it is time to build alternatives. Alternatives are the detailed plans for resolving the causes of the problem. When considering alternatives, it is important to be aware of the five types of actions available as the foundation for decision making—adaptive, interim, contingent, corrective, and preventive:

- **Adaptive action** means living with the present problem. The company has no control or influence over certain business requirements, such as taxes, the price of utilities, the weather, overseas competition, and material prices at the point of manufacturing.

- **Interim action** means doing something that is not currently being done as a stopgap before the final product or service is available. This includes leasing equipment while the current equipment is being repaired or hiring temporary help during peak periods.

- If something can go wrong, it probably will. A customer may change plans, a key employee might take a job with a competitor. Being able to react with a "fix" is a **contingent action**.

- **Corrective action** means returning to the intended condition, such as, replacing a burned-out fuse or oiling a noisy hinge.

- **Preventive action** means looking into the immediate, short-term, midterm, and long-term future for potential problems.

By taking preventive action and analyzing potential problems, you anticipate future situations and engage in the problem-solving/decision-making process to develop alternatives and take action before a problem occurs. The alternatives may include clearly articulating the desired end results and gaining understanding, acceptance, and support (UAS) from everyone affected. Furthermore, the alternatives may include developing the task that sets in motion the work to be done to accomplish the desired end results, keeping in mind the basic format of a task:

- Activities include the who, what, where, when, cost, and so on. This includes gaining UAS with everyone who participates in the work.

- Value means that efforts are clearly worthy and competitive, which adds to the bottom line. When people UAS the value of their work to the business, they more readily accept their responsibility, authority, and accountability for successfully attaining the desired end results.

- Looking at the conditions for success, sometimes others are needed, as well as additional technical and financial resources, to get the job done.

It is important that others have understanding, acceptance, and support (UAS) for their part of the task before the work begins. This helps them plan their participation in the work. The problem-solving and decision-making format using the UAS-SEA approach helps people think through the specifics of the work in relation to the stated desired end results. Adopting this problem-solving and decision-making approach is an interdependent discipline within the business that warrants absolute commitment.

Indeed, decisions have a greater chance of being implemented when alternatives are developed with this process in effect as a standard business practice. Failure to analyze potential problems and make clear decisions affects employee motivation and physical and financial resources and encourages subpar work that affects all stakeholders. Using UAS-SEA for problem solving and decision making is a *magnificent obsession*.

Summary

In this chapter, we examined the Work/Life Approach to time management and problem solving. In particular, we looked at the following:

- The prioritizing and time management matrix
- The situation-expectation-action (SEA) approach to focusing on the root cause of the problem
- Problem solving and decision making using UAS

Moreover, you saw how the Work/Life Approach focuses on the vital few while being responsible for eliminating the trivial many, and how people focus on the work to achieve the desired end results.

Keep in mind the importance of getting understanding, acceptance, and support (UAS) from everyone involved and focusing on the root cause. Consider what would happen if you didn't use the prioritizing and time management or the SEA Work/Life Approaches.

In Chapter 9, we introduce the Work/Life Approach to resolving issues and working in teams to create a professional workplace environment.

9

Why Play the Blame Game?

Why play the blame game? Think about the implications of this statement. In Chapter 5, we discussed a production problem that Fusch (2001a) discovered, in which a worker, lead, and supervisors worked together and found a solution. Within about 30 minutes, they prevented the problem from reoccurring, and they avoided making accusations and blaming for creating the problem. Fusch found that, by embracing the Work/Life Approach, Western Manufacturing had avoided the blame game and potential downtime and losses.

Finding fault and assigning blame is part of the human condition because of the depravity of human beings. In business, problems, challenges, and differences in perspective are everyday occurrences. Some can create considerable loss, not to mention the potential health impact from anxiety, anger, and stress. This Work/Life Approach builds on understanding, acceptance, and support (UAS) and situation, expectations, and actions (SEA) to create a Conversation Without Blame (CWB).

Following the Conversation Without Blame Work/Life Approach to resolving issues, illustrated in Figure 9.1, we provide points for everyone involved in the conversation to reflect on. Beginning with self-assessment and analyzing the situation, participants in the conversation need to focus on identifying the desired end result and communicate to resolve issues to reach the desired end result.

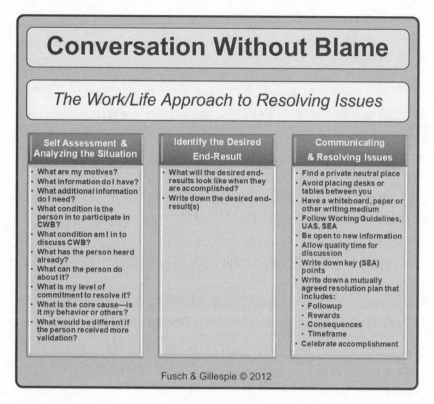

Figure 9.1 Conversation Without Blame Work/Life Approach

Self Assessment and Analyzing the Situation

To conduct a self-assessment and analyze the situation, each person in the conversation needs to reflect and ask himself or herself the following questions:

- **What are my motives?** This is perhaps the most critical question! This question often takes much introspection and is pivotal to resolving issues. If you do not understand your motives, you have no reason to argue. When people understand their own motives, it is easier to focus on the work and look at issues from different perspectives.

- **What relevant, valid, timely, and reliable (RVTR) information do I have?** If I do not have all the useful information, I cannot argue a point or have a conversation about an issue.

- **What additional RVTR information do I need?** After analyzing the useful information you do have, you need to determine what useful information you still need to discuss and resolve an issue.

- **Is the person ready to participate in a Conversation Without Blame?** Sometimes people have external pressures and are unprepared to discuss and help resolve an issue. When people cannot actively participate in a discussion about an issue, it is best to postpone or reschedule the conversation. (In some cases this may require engaging a facilitator.)

- **Am I ready to participate in a Conversation Without Blame?** Sometimes you have external pressures and are unprepared to discuss and help resolve an issue. Likewise, when you are in no condition to actively participate in a discussion about an issue, it is best to postpone or reschedule the conversation.

- **What has the person heard already?** Under the Work/Life Approach, we argue for sharing useful information. We also argue that superfluous information and rumors are devastating to a business. It is important to clarify what the person has already heard to correct any misinformation.

- **What can the person do about the issue?** In other words, if an issue is beyond a person's control, there may be no positive result from having a conversation about the issue. Consider this adage: Don't shoot the messenger.

- **What is my level of commitment to resolving the issue?** If you are not fully committed to addressing and resolving an issue, you must ask yourself why you are expending the energy.

- **What is the core cause? Is it my behavior or others'?** This is an important reflection. Without realizing it, you may have in fact been the cause of the issue.

- **What would be different if the person received more validation?** Validations are important. A lack of deserved validation affects people in different ways.

These self-assessment questions are critical to ask yourself before beginning a conversation to resolve an issue. After all the participants in the conversation have gone through the self-reflection and introspective questions phase, it is important to identify what the desired end result from the conversation should look like. Ask about and write down the desired end results for all the participants in the conversation:

- **What will the desired end results look like when they are accomplished?** As we have shown in several of the Work/Life Approaches throughout this book, it is vital to describe what the desired end results of any activity will look like when accomplished. Otherwise, there will be no way to identify what has been accomplished.

After the participants in the conversation have gone through the self-assessment, analyzed the situation, and identified what the desired end result from the conversation should look like, it is time to communicate and resolve the issues. To do so, follow these steps:

- **Find a private or neutral place.** It is important that there are not distractions and that people do not involve themselves in conversation in passing—particularly because other people may not have all the information.
- **Avoid placing desks or tables between you.** It is important to not have barriers to fixate on while you are working together to resolve the issues.
- **Have a whiteboard, paper, computer, or other writing medium.** This is important to help visualize the issues.
- **Follow Working Guidelines, UAS, and SEA.** As we discussed in Chapter 3, when Working Guidelines are used

correctly, the organization increases the flow of useful information, values people, and enhances the quality of work and Work/Life. Likewise, understanding, acceptance, and support (UAS) and situation, expectations, and actions (SEA) are critical to provide a Conversation Without Blame.

- **Be open to new information.** Frequently you do not have all the information. It is important to be open to new information that may provide a good rationale to look at an issue from a different perspective.

- **Allow quality time for discussion.** Different people have different values, ideas, and passions that lead to diversity in perspectives. It is important to give each person in the conversation time to communicate their perspective and share in resolving the issues.

- **Write down key SEA points.** Recall the problem-solving and decision-making process we discussed in Chapter 8. Identifying what should be going on (WSBGO), what is going on (WIGO), and the problem gap is vital to identifying and solving a problem.

- **Write down a mutually agreed-upon resolution plan that includes the following:**

  - **Follow-up.** How will the follow-up activities occur, and who will take responsibility? In other words, who owns it?

  - **Rewards.** What will be potential rewards for positively solving the issues? This may be validation and recognition; it does not necessary mean financial.

  - **Consequences.** What are the consequences if the mutually agreed-upon resolution activities are not completed?

  - **Timeframe.** In what amount of time must the activities to reach the resolution be completed?

- **Celebrate accomplishment.** Whether resolving an issue was a small or large accomplishment, celebrating will encourage people to embrace the process of Conversation Without Blame to resolve issues in the future.

Throughout the CWB process, it is important to be a good listener, seek opportunities for solutions, and write down and clarify the points before leaving the meeting. Writing down the points and resolution plan eliminates convenient loss of memory (CLM) syndrome. When it is not written down, the resolution can be forgotten during the busy work shift. Writing it down clarifies the resolution plan and responsibilities. When following up on CWB, it is important to catch people doing things right and validate their actions. Providing positive feedback is a form of providing useful information without blame.

Similar to the Conversation Without Blame Work/Life Approach to resolving problems, people are frequently asked or directed to participate on teams to find solutions to various business challenges. Some teams find that they have difficulty getting started or in fact never get started. This tends to be a nonproductive use of time. As Senge (1990) noted, other teams develop a synergy in which the whole is greater than the parts (1 + 1 = 3 or more). In other words, some teams are highly productive, feed ideas off each other, and quickly achieve desired end results. The Work/Life Approach provides a dynamic Team/Group Project Guideline (see Figure 9.2) to help teams get off to a rapid start, focus on the tasks, and reach desired end results.

The Team/Group Project Guideline begins with a couple of foundational notations such as the title, a brief overview ("elevator speech") description of the project, and a list of the team/group members. The guideline provides seven columns that help teams focus on the project:

- The first column contains sequential numbers to help keep the tasks organized.
- In the second column, the team describes what the desired end results should look like when the project is complete.

Team/Group Project Guidelines

Project Synopsis: A succinct elevator speech type overview of the project

Team/Group Members						
	Desired End-Results	Current Information	Information Needed	Task to Acquire Information	Team/Group Member Assigned	Deadline for Task
1						
2						
3						
4						
5						
6						
7						
8						
9						
10						
11						
12						

- What is the plan for gaining Understanding, Acceptance, and Support (UAS)?

- Who will maintain this team/group activity master?

- Who will be responsible for compiling the information once the tasks are complete?

- How and when will the team/group members present the information?

Fusch & Gillespie © 2012

Figure 9.2 Team/Group Project Guidelines

- The third column lists the current useful information that the team members have.
- The fourth column asks the team to identify the useful information that will be needed to achieve the desired end results.

- The fifth column addresses the tasks needed to acquire the useful information described in the fourth column.

- The sixth column prompts the team to assign responsibility for each of the tasks.

- The seventh column specifies the deadline by which the team member assigned to a specific task will commit to complete the task.

The final requirements are as follows:

- The team should develop a UAS plan.

- Specify who will maintain the master project guideline and ensure that all the tasks are completed in a timely manner.

- Specify who will be responsible for compiling the information or assembling the project as soon as all the tasks are completed.

- Describe how and when the team will package and present the project.

Indeed, by using the Work/Life Approach to team and/or group projects, working teams can come together, quickly focus on the task at hand, and create synergy while maximizing team performance.

Summary

This chapter began with a powerful title. We described the dynamic Work/Life Approach to Conversations Without Blame (CWB) to resolve issues. The blame game devours the human assets of a business, reduces productivity, lowers morale, can cause illness both physical and mental, hurts the bottom line and stockholder equity, and drives away good people. CWB implemented well is a powerful tool for overall continuous improvement for the business. CWB is an investment; the blame game is a liability. The choice is yours!

Building on the CWB Work/Life Approach, this chapter introduced the Team/Group Project Guideline to help teams get a rapid start, focus on the tasks, and reach the desired end results.

In Chapter 10, we describe the Work/Life Approach to succeeding in the global economy by fostering change to enhance end results.

10

Fostering Change to Enhance
End Results

At the surface level, people address change in three ways. Some embrace change, others resist change, and still others look around and wonder what happened. Plato suggested that the only constant is change. Looking at the past, it is clear that change is inevitable and that not all change is within an individual or organization's control.

In Chapter 7, we discussed how stress is often beyond the individual's control. Likewise, many changes that occur are beyond an individual's control. However, it is how you address and influence change that *is* within your control that can make a difference at work, at home, and in society. Indeed, the choices you make can change your life. The actions of the present impact the future. Consider whether your present time is being *spent* or *invested*.

Spending time (metaphorically, *killing time*) means doing activities that have little lasting value. For example, spent time that has little to no long-term value may include activities such as watching television, gossiping, and dwelling on past mistakes that drain energy from the present.

In contrast to spending time in nonproductive ways, investing time in productive ways leads to positive change and desired end results. Investing time in developing habits that oppose distractions provides the foundation for change that leads to desired end results. Investing time also means maximizing every waking hour, focusing on work at home and in business that continually moves toward lasting change.

Change Management

In Chapter 1, we introduced the holistic performance improvement model (see Figure 10.1). It described the continual process of performance analysis, gap analysis, intervention selection, evaluation performance assessment strategy, intervention implementation, and evaluation performance assessment. It is a powerful change management model.

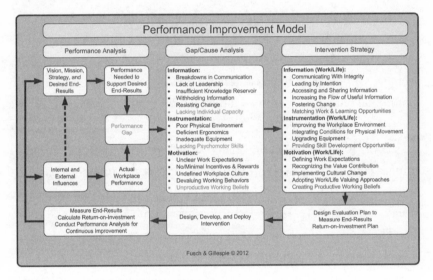

Figure 10.1 Performance improvement model

Specifically addressing change, the Work/Life Approach suggests a change management model that builds on the past and analyzes the present to move into the future (see Figure 10.2). Beginning with a comprehensive analysis of the business needs, the Work/Life Approach to change management suggests that there is a gap in the present and recent past between what is going on and what should be going on to obtain the desired end results in behavior, performance, and productivity.

During the planning and design phase, organizations seek to design the initiative that will best address the business needs for the future (immediate, near, short-term, and distant). As organizational leaders prepare to implement a change initiative, the initiative should be clearly communicated to all the stakeholders. Understanding, acceptance, and support (UAS) should be obtained so that people will understand the reason for the change and how they can contribute to realizing the desired end results.

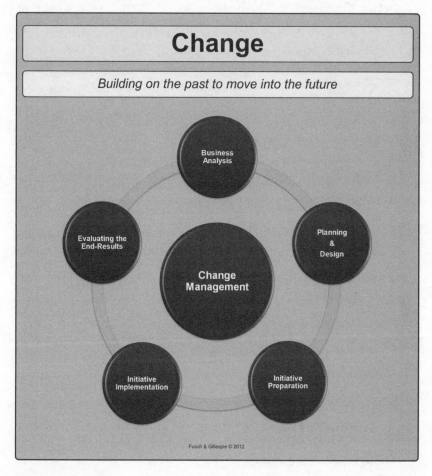

Figure 10.2 Change

With the exception of a reduction in force, the implementation phase should be rolled out with support of the people the change affects. With UAS, the people involved in the change initiative can make a positive impact. On the other hand, people who are not committed to the change can undermine the initiative's success. As with the Work/Life Performance Improvement Model, the Change Model requires that initiatives be evaluated to ensure that the desired end results were met. If they weren't, the evaluation should identify what change is needed to realize the desired end results.

Before the change initiative can begin, it is important to recognize and overcome resistance to change. Often people hold on to the past and resist change, thinking or arguing that the change will be worse than the present condition.

Resistance to Change

In addition to spending (killing) time on activities that have little lasting value, people resist change by doing the following:

- Finding fault with and blaming others for memories that are no longer relevant, valid, timely, and reliable (RVTR)
- Maintaining habits that get in the way of being the best they can be, such as smoking, excessive drinking, using drugs, violating driving laws, and practicing devaluing behaviors
- Labeling people with negative comments
- Fostering negative beliefs

Fostering negative beliefs includes arguments to avoid participating in change initiatives:

- Old people can't change.
- There is no place in business for sharing feelings.
- People don't want to change.
- Get rid of people in business if they disagree with their boss.
- Don't share ideas without concrete evidence that credit will be given.

- I distrust people until they have earned my trust.

- What goes around comes around.

- Everybody is in it for themselves.

- If I don't care about myself, no one else will either.

- The world is a cesspool, so watch where you step.

- It's a dog-eat-dog world.

- I will never find a decent place to work.

- Management will never truly share the wealth of the business.

- Stockholders will never realize that they should treat employees as their most important asset.

- Competition is the enemy.

In business, leaders look at ways to influence change to bring about the desired end results. Moreover, the Work/Life Approach uses UAS, validation, and valuing behaviors and commits to sharing only useful information (relevant, valid, timely, and reliable) to help people focus on positive behaviors that support change in the workplace. Keep in mind that the most critical ingredient for change is trust. Also keep in mind, as we discussed in Chapter 6, that trust is developed by increasing the flow of useful information and valuing behavior. There is no substitute for these two elements when increasing trust.

Change is always a dynamic effort to act differently and/or be different from what is occurring in the present. To be committed to change, you must recognize the value of continuous improvement in people's personal and work lives. The Work/Life Approach for helping people get to the point of commitment as an organizational leader and/or individual emphasizes the following process:

- Clearly document the specific *concern* that is triggering the need for change. Is it technical, administrative, financial, external, internal, personal, or corporate?

- Identify someone in the business who exhibits devaluing behavior as a normal way of engaging others. Analyze and describe that person's work behavior in specific, observable terms. After the concern for that devaluing behavior is UASed, select a specific idea for handling that devaluing behavior. One concept to consider is the Work/Life Approach to valuing behaviors, described in Chapter 6.

- Meet with the person, and review the Work/Life Approach to valuing behaviors as it pertains to his or her devaluing behavior. Such a confrontation provides that person with specific, useful information about areas to work on, with ongoing follow-up activity.

- Frequent follow-up demonstrating improvement will help the person understand that this way of working is of real value to the person as an individual and also is of value to the company.

- As the person experiences success, commitment for continuing this change in behavior becomes real and lasting change. The term for this is *intrinsic motivation*. Change has become a part of the person's fiber.

A concept provides people with useful information that helps them learn additional ways to implement the change process. Just saying "You have to change your behavior" is of little value. Teaching the person *how* is of lasting value. This approach is called the five C's of change (see Figure 10.3).

The sequence starts with a *concern* and then moves on to *concept*. From there you have a *confrontation* to validate the use of the concept. Implementing the concept over time develops a *conviction* that the concept is worthwhile and gains intrinsic *commitment* to make lasting change.

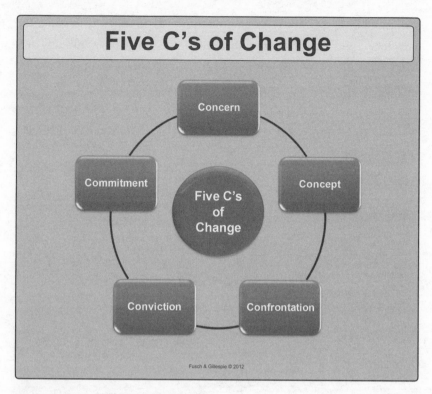

Figure 10.3 The five C's of change

Although it looks simple, this idea takes work. This book has never stated that creating a performance culture is easy. For change to be done properly, it is important to *maintain continuity with the past while moving into the future.* Five elements help change occur, and the same five elements get in the way of change: *memories, habits, labeling, beliefs,* and *visions* (see Figure 10.4). Each of these elements has a positive and negative impact on change.

Memories

Positive memories encourage change, and negative memories get in the way of change. Therefore, people should build on their positive memories. Clearly identify your negative memories, and then develop a definitive plan to try to create a positive experience to replace the negative memories that are still alive. This approach eventually suffocates the negative memories. It is not uncommon to find examples of people holding on to negative memories for 20 or more years, and these memories fester throughout the business. Think of all the wasted opportunities for creating a fun place to work in that business.

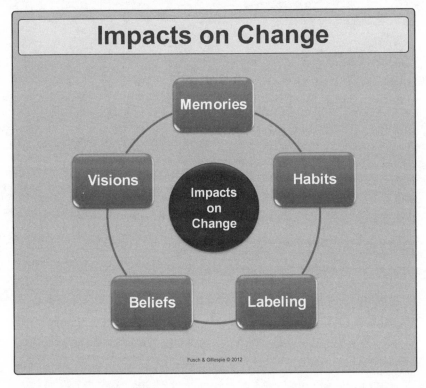

Figure 10.4 Impacts on change

Habits

A habit is something that people keep doing—sometimes without realizing they are still doing it. It is important to periodically take inventory of people's positive and negative habits. Positive habits encourage change; negative habits get in the way of change. Building on positive habits is an opportunity few people even consider, because their positive habits are not at the forefront of their minds. It is important to take inventory of positive habits and consider ways to increase their value. It is also important to catch people doing things right and validate good habits. Better yet, consider the potential results if people in the workplace catch each other doing things right and continually validate good habits and behaviors.

The benefits of identifying and focusing on good habits are evident. Therefore, let's explore some ways to replace bad habits with good habits. Over the years we have developed the habit of being on time for appointments—actually, being early. Sharing the benefits of this habit has encouraged others to adopt it too.

Some people have the negative habit of jumping to conclusions before performing due diligence and getting the facts. Sharing the Work/Life Approach to problem solving gives people a means to stop jumping to conclusions. Jumping to conclusions is a clear sign of premature closure. Premature closure means making decisions as though you know what you're doing, even with insufficient information and limited understanding.

One of the most devastating habits that owners and executives in the workplace can exhibit is an inability to behave in a manner that values people and fosters increasing the flow of useful information. Examples of poor behavior include putting people down, verbal abuse, pounding on furniture, using bad language, not listening to the whole story, and interrupting subordinates. It is a wonder that businesses operated by people who exhibit these kinds of behaviors continue to exist. One answer is that people put up with this poor habitual behavior because they need the job. But businesses often lose good people who won't put up with this type of behavior.

Owners and executives who behave this way have given themselves license to do so under the theory that it is their prerogative. Their philosophy is "I'm in charge" and/or "It's my business." All too often this philosophy is ingrained in a poor manager's habitual pattern of work behavior.

Some owners and executives have not been confronted with the ramifications of this type of behavior because their people lack the knowledge, skill, experience, and competence to undertake Conversation Without Blame. We have found that most owners and executives who behave poorly willingly try to change their devaluing behavior when given Work/Life tools to replace their negative habits with positive ones.

Labeling

The labeling element of change could include people's like or dislike of certain products and services. Some people refuse to buy a foreign car, a Ford owner wouldn't buy a Dodge, and so on. Some people avoid shopping at a particular store because they once experienced poor service there, and they readily share that opinion with others. In fact, our observations have shown that negative opinions about an organization travel as much as ten times faster than positive opinions.

Although we could spend considerable time discussing how bad news about an organization travels faster than good news, this topic is beyond the scope of this book. The labeling being considered here is the labeling of people. Labeling people at work is an ancient practice. Positive labels value people; negative labels devalue people.

In business, people are labeled constantly as they are being considered for continuing employment or promotion or when work is slacking off and a reduction in force is imminent. Performance reviews can encompass both current performance and historical labeling from past performance. All too often labeling is based on information received from others, not on behavior that was personally observed. You should always make an effort to verify that what you hear or read is useful information (relevant, valid, timely, and reliable) regardless of the source.

People are to each other what their shared experiences have been. This includes the distant past as well as the recent past. Also remember that just because information comes from a friend doesn't mean it is automatically useful or accurate, and the reverse is also true. Information that focuses on the work is the best kind of information when evaluating performance. When you focus on the work, it is easier to be more specific and to minimize other people's agendas. It is important to periodically take time to review how you have labeled people. It is best to erase labels and refresh your mental vision. People change, and they deserve our best efforts to stay up to date.

Negative labeling can get in the way of change, and positive labeling facilitates change. Beware of gossip and those who practice this behavior! This is best handled by ensuring that conversations focus on the work and offer useful information.

Beliefs

The Work/Life Approach to change suggests that you focus on Working Beliefs rather than political, economic, social, or religious beliefs. Focusing on the work increases the flow of useful information and helps you value people.

All the ideas in the Work/Life Approach to getting things done are a collection of Working Beliefs that disregard race, creed, color, religion, sex, and age. When businesses commit to the Work/Life Approach for getting things done, they make these Working Beliefs visible in thought, word, and deed. The end result is acquiring wealth to gain additional capital to grow and prosper and doing so in valuing ways. Sharing personal Working Beliefs with others helps foster a commitment to work interdependently.

Vision

Vision is the last and most important element of the impacts on change. A vision is a thought process that looks into the future and pictures the desired future condition. Positive visions create energy;

negative visions consume energy. Businesses that constantly worry about today have little, if any, time to look into the future. They become managed by the present rather than managing. When a business is operationally sound, the assumptions for the future are realistic and provide the direction and movement for focusing on immediate, near-term, short-term, and distant end results. Not having the operational basics in place is a prescription for failure. The Work/Life Approach to change supports the idea that the business is operationally sound when it values its people, focuses on the work, and believes in the sharing of useful information (relevant, valid, timely, and reliable).

The *Art of Visioning* is the most important catalyst for continuous improvement. Continuous improvement can occur only through a deliberate commitment to understanding change as a lifelong process founded on the following:

- Mastering the basics of getting things done—in other words, always focusing on the business's strategic and operational work.
- Having UAS about the business's present operational condition. This also means having UAS for the business's desired strategic future condition.

Visions provide hope, excitement, and energy. The more clear the vision, the more hope, excitement, and energy are created. The dilemma for many businesses is the propensity to treat visioning as an occasional task. This occurs because there is no conceptual framework for simply placing visions in a category that allows for differing degrees of clarity and a place in time. Not all visions start out clear, nor is there always time to handle them all right now. Here is a simple way to handle these variables:

- Foggy (long-term) visions in the "thinking out loud" stage are at 1 to 5 on the scale of 1 to 20, where commitment is at 20.

- Misty (midterm) visions in the "thinking out loud" stage are at a 6 to 10 on the 1-to-20 scale.

- Partly cloudy (short-term) visions in the "thinking out loud" stage are at 11 to 15 on the 1-to-20 scale.

- Clear (ready to use as resources are available) visions in the "thinking out loud" stage are at 16 to 20 on the 1-to-20 scale.

Moving a clear vision from the strategic side of the business to the operational side is an ongoing iterative process affected by the current resources and timing. The foggy, misty, and partly cloudy visions that are being worked on in the present are in the strategic arena of management. The strategic arena holds ideas that are not ready to be implemented in daily operations.

At this point in the book, you might conclude that maintaining continuity with the past as you move into the future takes a lot of work. Anything less than what the Work/Life Approach advocates exponentially reduces the opportunity for continuous improvement. Indeed, individual behavioral change in business depends on the person's desire to focus on the work, share useful information, value others, and persevere in attaining the end results that the business has hired the person to achieve.

Motivation to make lasting change comes from within the person (it's intrinsic). People are unable to change other people. However, organizational leaders can provide opportunities for people to change by being clear about the desired end results and providing consistent feedback to the person doing the work.

Furthermore, because most people are not psychiatrists, they should be cautious and avoid explaining people's failure to change or negative behavior as a lack of self-esteem. By continuously focusing on the work, following the Work/Life Approach to UAS, and providing validation and quality Conversation Without Blame, people help people enhance their motivation and self-esteem as a direct result of doing a good job. If this doesn't work, suggest that they undergo counseling, or assist them in finding new career opportunities outside the organization.

It is important to maintain continuity with the past as the organization moves into the future. However, remember that the elements that both help and hinder change are memories, habits, labeling, beliefs, and visions. Change takes time. For some people there is *never time to do it right and always time to do it over*. But it is important that this philosophy be laid to rest.

Summary

In this book's Preface, we asked you to imagine a utopian workplace and suggested that the Work/Life Approach can help lead an organization in that direction (see Figure 10.5). In our work with organizations that strive to adhere to the Work/Life Approach, we have seen substantial success. We leave you with these final thoughts:

- Envision a place where people strive for continuous improvement.
- Envision a place where people communicate clearly.
- Envision a place where people freely share information.
- Envision a place where people understand one another.
- Envision a place where people feel that they make a difference.
- Envision a place where people respect those they work for.
- Envision a place where people want to spend their time.
- Envision a place where people have fun every day.
- Envision a place where people share the rewards both financially and emotionally based on their contributions.

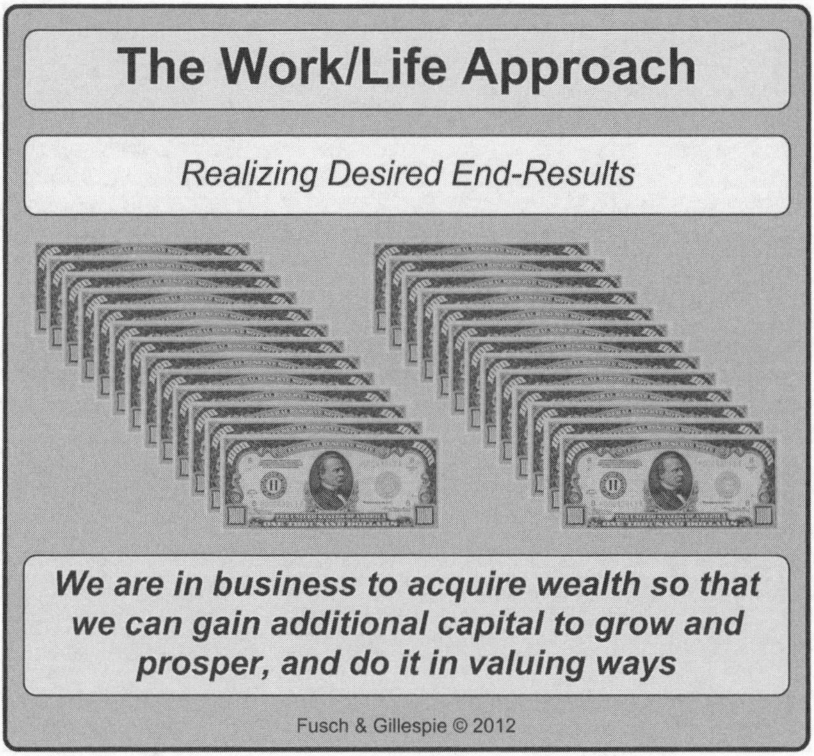

Figure 10.5 The Work/Life Approach to realizing desired end results

In this book's Preface, we suggested that you ask yourself this question: If I do not accept these ideas, *what is the alternative?* In conclusion, have you UASed today?

Measuring End Results:
The Return-on-Investment Plan

After you have selected an intervention strategy to reduce the gap between the needed performance to obtain the desired end results and the actual workplace performance, it is important to design an evaluation measurement strategy (see Figure A.1). Doing so helps you figure out when the desired performance has been met. This appendix discusses scientific methods (using both hard data, such as records, and soft data, such as people's perspectives) you can use to evaluate the results of an intervention and measure the return on investment (ROI). Let's start by reviewing the origins of measuring the ROI for performance interventions.

In the beginning, intervention evaluation was most prominent in the training classroom when evaluation was desired. Unfortunately, most training evaluation encompassed (and still does) what performance professionals call "smiley face evaluation." This is a brief questionnaire at the end of the training session that asks the participants if they liked the course, if they liked the facility, if they liked the instructor, and if the coffee and donuts were good. In other words, did the participants have fun, and do they want to do it again? From a measurement perspective, such a questionnaire would confirm for performance and human resources development professionals that the workers like or do not like to take time away from their jobs to sit in a classroom and enjoy a presentation, coffee, and donuts. What we do not know is if the training intervention had a positive impact on the desired end results.

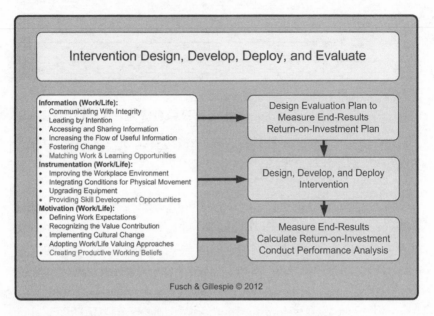

Figure A.1 Intervention design, develop, deploy, and evaluate

Interest is growing in results-based performance improvement interventions that are linked to the organization's strategic plan. This is visible through the interest in going beyond the traditional four steps for evaluating training programs (assessing the reaction, learning, behavior, and results) and calculating the ROI for training (Bartel, 2000; Hale, 1998; Kirkpatrick, 2006; Phillips, 1997, 2011; Stolovitch and Maurice, 1998). Indeed, since the 1990s, Jack Phillips and Patricia Phillips have written over 50 books on calculating the ROI for training. Phillips (1997, 2011) provided a detailed model to evaluate all stages of the training program and emphasized a strategy for calculating the ROI, as shown in Figure A.2.

In a like manner, Hale (1998) developed a strategy for conducting task analysis, evaluating the performance intervention to identify the internal or external performance improvement consultant's value. She provided two models to show how human performance technologists can go beyond evaluation levels 1, 2, 3, and 4 (Kirkpatrick, 2006).

The first model points out four elements of job or task analysis and how to measure each one:

- Inputs are the resources such as information, equipment, and people needed to perform the job or task.
- Processes are the activities that make up the job or task.
- Outputs are the products of the processes.
- Outcomes are the results of the outputs vis-à-vis costs, satisfaction, accomplishment, and image.

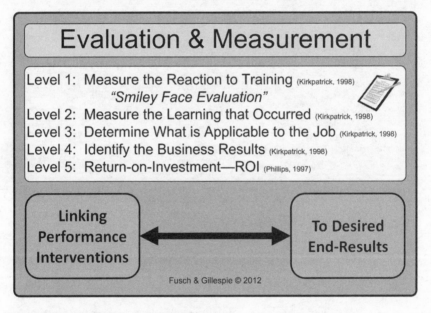

Figure A.2 Evaluation and measurement

Hale's (1998) second model metaphorically resembles a road map that helps the performance technologist navigate each stage of the performance and/or training intervention development process. Indeed, emerging from training, performance improvement strategies have embraced the ROI methods to measure all performance interventions and ensure that the desired end results have been met.

We argue that an ROI strategy should always be employed before the design, development, and deployment of a performance intervention. Doing so ensures that the best intervention was selected and that the intervention is designed to bring the desired end results. Indeed, as Covey (2004) maintained that one should always begin with the end in mind, we too have always considered the desired end result before initiating any performance intervention. So to begin with the end in mind, we will walk through our five-step ROI process, shown in Figure A.3.

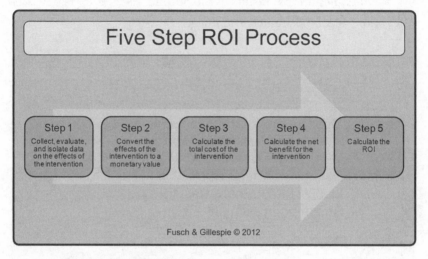

Figure A.3 Five-step ROI process

Our ROI model involves five basic steps that seem simple yet also complex:

1. Collect, evaluate, and isolate tangible and intangible data concerning the effects of a performance intervention.

2. Convert the isolated effects of a performance intervention into a monetary value.

3. Calculate the total cost of a performance intervention.

4. Calculate the net benefit of a performance intervention by subtracting the total performance intervention costs from the total performance intervention benefits.

5. Calculate the ROI by dividing the net performance intervention benefits from step 4 by the training program costs from step 3 and then multiplying the product by 100.

The literature provides numerous case studies and detailed descriptions of the ROI process for determining the effectiveness of a performance intervention. As shown in our model, the math and five-step ROI process appear linear and simple. However, sometimes peculiarities hinder an organization's data collection for an ROI process. To overcome these barriers to data collection, we employ the scientific method of hypothetical-deductive reasoning to evaluate the effectiveness of the intervention. The following sections explain some of the methodology we use to determine the program costs and to measure the effects of the performance intervention. These methods may be used by organizations with similar issues.

Step 1: Collect, Evaluate, and Isolate Data on the Effects of the Intervention

The first step in this model involves collecting data on the effects of a performance intervention. Before a performance intervention is implemented, the total performance intervention cost and the projected benefits of the intervention should be estimated. Through such planning, you can simulate the results of a proposed performance intervention and logically speculate on the value of the performance intervention in relation to the ROI. Following this logic, the cost should be calculated during the planning stage.

However, this discussion follows the sequence of the ROI formula. It begins by isolating the effects of performance intervention and leaves the (already calculated) performance intervention cost to step 3 (Fusch, 2008). Figure A.4 shows some of the best potential end results from a successful performance intervention.

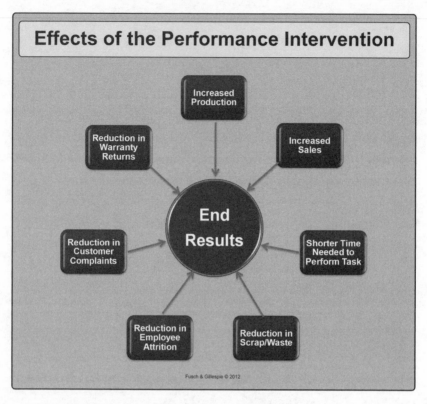

Figure A.4 Effects of the performance intervention

Numerous scientific methods can be used to measure the effects of an intervention. Phillips (1997, 2011) from a training perspective suggested that companies that follow best practices analyze each specific situation and select the best methods to collect the data needed to measure training. Some of the more common methods that we support include measuring an intervention's impact on the following:

- Increased worker/employee/team production
- Increased sales performance
- Shorter time required to perform a task
- Reduction in waste, scrap, or the rework rate
- Reduction in employee attrition

- Reduction in customer complaints
- Reduction in warranty work or customer returns

To measure the potential effects of a performance intervention, you may use changes in performance indicators such as production reports, sales reports, time-per-task records, tardiness and absentee records, human resources management and staffing records, customer service phone calls and time addressing customer calls, and warranty and customer return records.

To address these different end results from an intervention, Phillips (1997, 2011) argued for traditional research methods and used data collection methods to determine the effects of a performance intervention in the early stages of an ROI process: surveys, questionnaires, interviews, focus groups, tests, observation, and performance records. In an examination of these methods, it is clear that organizational performance records are most credible if the particular method is feasible. Following the organizational performance records methodology, supervisors of employees participating in an intervention are often good sources of data. Third-party observation may produce valuable information but can be cost-prohibitive. Information collected directly from the performance intervention participants can also produce valuable results. Phillips (1997, 2011) supported using multiple data collection methods to ensure that the results were not caused by an external element. For instance, suppose the organizational performance records indicate a substantial increase in production after a particular performance intervention. The supervisors and performance intervention participants suggest little change in individual performance. Or perhaps the performance intervention had no relationship to the job tasks. In this case it is possible that the increase in production was caused by some external effect such as a new technology. Similar to analyzing the effects of an intervention, in sociological research, Denzin (1970, 2009) coined the term *triangulation*. This means that the researcher uses multiple sources of information or collection methods to ascertain the meaning of the phenomenon. From a mathematical perspective, triangulation means using three points to identify one precise central point. The validity of the process may be enhanced by multiple sources of information. Denzin (1970, 2009) identified four types of triangulation. Data triangulation encompasses getting data through different sampling strategies. Investigator triangulation involves correlating data from multiple researchers. Theoretical triangulation uses different theoretical perspectives to gather data. Methodological triangulation includes more than one method for collecting data. This leaves the question of which method or methods would work best for an organization's evaluation and ROI strategy (Fusch, 2008). For measuring the effects of performance interventions, we found that using Denzin's (1970, 2009) methodological triangulation strategy by correlating multiple sources of data to learn the effects of a performance intervention enhances the validity of the results.

In some instances, an entire workforce participates in the performance intervention. When all workers in the organization or all workers in a particular division, department, or team participate in the intervention, using organizational performance records is the leading information collection method. However, when a performance intervention is for a specific individual or individuals spread across an organization, isolating the effects of the intervention can be challenging. Following the Phillips (1997, 2011) and Denzin (1970, 2009) arguments, the following soft-data collection strategies provide multiple sources to enhance validity when hard-data performance indicators such as production records, sales records, and time records are unavailable:

- Post-initiative questionnaires are given to the participants at the end of their participation in the initiative and at specific intervals after the intervention, such as every month or every six months.

- Coworker questionnaires are given shortly after the worker/ employee participates in the initiative and at specific intervals after the intervention.
- Supervisor questionnaires are given shortly after the worker/ employee participates in the initiative and at specific intervals after the intervention.
- Direct observation offers considerable value, but it takes time and requires a performance professional.
- Participants are interviewed at the end of their participation in the initiative and at specific intervals after the intervention.
- The participants' supervisors are interviewed shortly after the worker/employee participates in the initiative and at specific intervals after the intervention.
- The participants' coworkers are interviewed shortly after the worker/employee participates in the initiative and at specific intervals after the intervention.
- The participants' customers, vendors, and supply chain are interviewed as appropriate.
- The participants or their supervisors participate in focus groups at specific intervals after the intervention.

Employing this methodology and isolating the effects of the performance intervention by considering all the data can provide a credible measurement for an ROI strategy. Also, when using soft methods (people's perspectives) to measure the impact of a performance initiative, it is important to triangulate (Denzin, 1970, 2009) and to correlate multiple sources of useful information (relevant, valid, timely, and reliable).

Participants' Post-Initiative Questionnaires

Although this is soft information, Phillips (1997, 2011) suggested a method of asking sales people how much they increased their performance and then how certain they were about their estimated results. We have discovered a similar good soft-data method. We ask a question related to a performance intervention—or, more frequently, a learning intervention—followed by asking the worker/employee how confident he is in his estimate. We have found that this is a good start on collecting data when hard-data performance indicators are unavailable. As we mentioned, most organizations do not measure performance interventions, and many organizations have not gone above Kirkpatrick's (2006) level 1 evaluation. Figure A.5 shows the types of questions that can address level 1, 2, 3, and 4 evaluations for learning interventions.

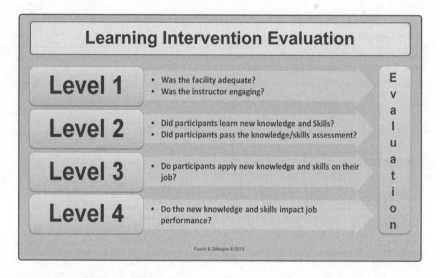

Figure A.5 Learning intervention evaluation

To address the effects of performance and learning interventions through soft-data questionnaires, we argue that the confidence model (see Figure A.6) and triangulating multiple sources of conservative soft data will enhance the validity and reliability of people's perspectives. Moreover, correlating multiple data sources provides useful information (relevant, valid, timely, and reliable) to identify the end results of a performance intervention.

Level 3 – Confidence Model

Using the new skills you have learned, how many more widgets will you be able to produce in a day?	5 □	10 □	15 □	20 □	Other ___

How sure you about your answer in the question above?	10% □	20% □	30% □	40% □	50% □
	60% □	70% □	80% □	90% □	100% □

Using the new skills you have learned, how much time will you be able to save per day?	15 min □	30 min □	45 min □	1 hour □	Other ___

How sure you about your answer in the question above?	10% □	20% □	30% □	40% □	50% □
	60% □	70% □	80% □	90% □	100% □

Fusch & Gillespie © 2012

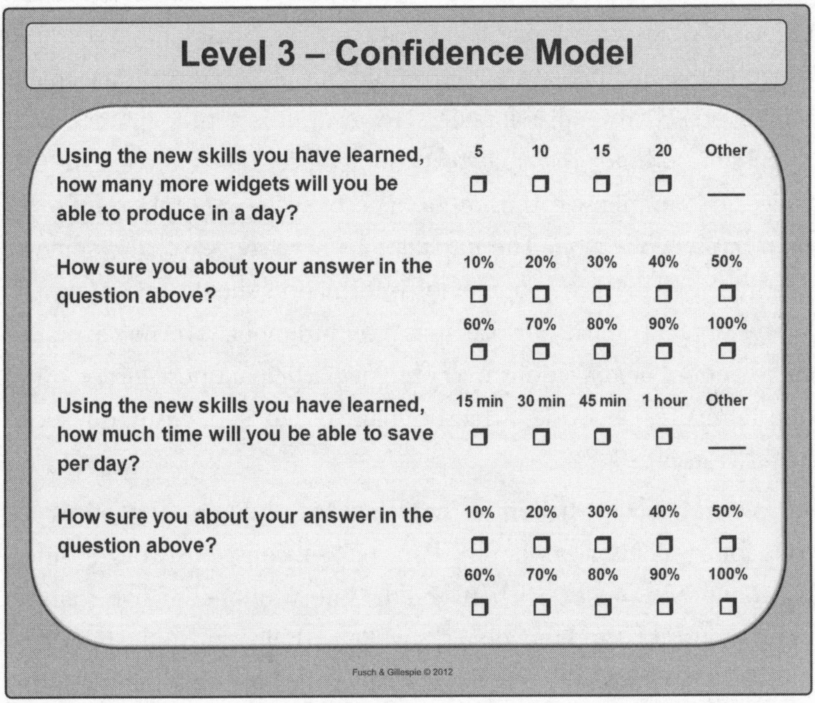

Figure A.6 Level 3: confidence model

The ability to e-mail a link to online questionnaires has made this method more desirable—as long as those who receive the questionnaire are tracked to ensure that they complete it. Multiplying the estimate of the effects of the intervention by the participant's certainty about the effect provides a conservative confidence figure on the effects of the performance intervention. Moreover, using Denzin's (1970, 2009) methodological triangulation strategy of correlating multiple sources of data such as participant questionnaires, coworker questionnaires, and supervisor questionnaires at selected times after the intervention can provide useful information and results (relevant, valid, timely, and reliable).

Although Phillips (1997, 2011) stressed that supervisors should be objective when completing the questionnaires, considerable research suggests that such an evaluation would be subjective and that maintaining objectivity is problematic. However, it is not the intent of this discussion to enter the objectivity-subjectivity debate. We note this concern to emphasize the importance of using multiple sources of information collection. The implications here suggest that whenever possible, two or three sources of information should be employed. When organizational performance measurements are not a practicable option, organizations may employ participant post-intervention questionnaires, coworker questionnaires, and supervisor questionnaires (Fusch, 2008).

A potential side benefit is that when the same questionnaires are used for every intervention, workers may subconsciously begin thinking about the connectivity between the interventions (such as training or using job aids) and the job tasks while participating in the intervention. This concept suggests that workers will remember the questionnaire and focus on concepts that may be related to their individual performance. This potential advantage is also a potential limitation. The limitation is that the participants may anticipate the questionnaire and answer how they believe the company wants them to answer, which may compromise its effectiveness. However, repeated use and confidentiality should reduce this potential limitation (Fusch 2008).

For a small number of workers, using questionnaires with the confidence model can provide organizations with a tool to overcome barriers to calculating a ROI for many of the ongoing performance initiatives. Consider that workers in nonsales roles such as those detailed by Phillips (1997) may have difficulty determining a monetary impact on the performance initiative. To resolve this issue, we suggest replacing a Phillips-type monetary question with questions related to saving time, increasing production, or reducing waste (Fusch, 2008).

Step 2: Convert the Effects of Performance Intervention into a Monetary Value

This potential to place a monetary value on the effects of a performance intervention can at first seem daunting. Let's review some methods to do so.

Direct Observation

Observation offers considerable value. A colleague often tells a story about the time he worked as a performance improvement technologist for a leading washing machine manufacturer. One of the manufacturing challenges was that the line kept slowing down due to one worker. Rather than continuing to pressure that worker, management asked our colleague to take a look at the problem. To analyze the problem from a performance improvement technologist perspective, our colleague took a folding chair to the factory and sat down and observed the worker for about 30 minutes. The worker, seeing the white hat (signifying management) on the performance improvement technologist, worked very hard to keep up during the 30 minutes, until the break whistle sounded. The worker asked why the technologist was watching him. The technologist answered, "I noticed that you have to lean way over to reach the part." The worker replied that he did, and that he went home with a sore back every day. As a result of this observation, two hydraulic rams were installed. One pushed the part directly in front of the worker on the assembly line, and another returned the part after the worker's task was completed. The direct end result after the intervention was that the line no longer slowed down at that location, and the worker was much happier and performed well on the job. Although this example was more of a performance analysis, the observation could also be used to follow up after the intervention to document the change in performance and to measure time savings or waste reduction. After identifying the benefits, you can convert them into a monetary value for the ROI calculation. You can measure the net profits from the change in performance, savings in wages and benefits resulting from time savings, or reductions in the cost or value of waste.

Interviews with Participants, Coworkers, and Supervisors

Chapter 5 described the Work/Life Approach to Sapiential Authority. Empowering people closest to the point of action to make decisions, make suggestions, and use their knowledge and judgment without being tied up in bureaucracy enhances performance. To find out what is going on, it is a good idea to interview participants to get their perspectives on the results of the initiative. (This is true even if they can only tell how much faster they work or how much more they can produce in a day.) Interviewing the people closest to the action helps determine what the actual change is and clarifies the potential cause of the intervention.

For example, suppose a new department manager purchases a new computer software package and provides training for the employees. Performance (production) improves shortly after the intervention. You might conclude that the training was what made the difference. Someone else might conclude that the new software made the difference. Interviewing the employees participating in the initiative might help you figure out whether the software or training made the difference. However, when you interview the people closest to the point of action, you might find that the change was due to the new department manager's validation of employees and her management style, which inspired people to perform better.

Likewise, Fusch (2008) noted about supervisor questionnaires that the employee's supervisor is a good source to interview to determine if a performance or change initiative made a difference in performance and, if so, how much of a difference. Similar to the participant interviews and supervisor interviews, the participants' coworkers also can reveal a change in performance.

As mentioned, after you identify the benefits, you can convert them into a monetary value for the ROI calculation by measuring the net profits from the change in performance, savings in wages and benefits resulting from time savings, or reductions in the cost or value of waste.

Interviews with Participants' Customers, Vendors, and Supply Chain as Appropriate

In today's workplace, organizational leaders frequently realize the value of partnering up and down the supply chain. Even within a large organization, Division A may be the customer of Division B. Interviewing the participants' customers, vendors, and supply chain can be a good way to determine a change in performance and productivity.

Focus Groups Can Add to the Synergy of a Group's Output

Often a critical analysis of a well facilitated focus group can quickly identify the amount of change in performance and can be more accurate than a particular individual.

Measuring a Change in Production

Performance indicators are a great source of hard data to evaluate the performance initiative. We suggest using a time-series methodology similar to Phillips' (1997, 2011) argument to measure changes in production/performance shortly (such as one month) after the performance intervention and again at a predetermined time (such as six months or a year) after the performance intervention. This helps you ascertain if the intervention will provide long-term results.

The formula for measuring the changes through performance indicators is a simple process of analyzing the daily/weekly/monthly Key Performance Indicators and finding any measurable changes in annual production/performance at predetermined times after the performance intervention. The following concerns should be carefully analyzed:

- What level does production maintain after a period of time (such as one month and again after six months)?
- What changes in production correspond to the participant and supervisor questionnaire results?
- What is the external effect for changes in production not related to the performance intervention (company policy or procedures, equipment, workplace environment, numbers of employees, pay incentives)?

If the concerns are unsubstantiated, and the changes in production correspond with the participant, coworker, and supervisor questionnaires, you may conclude that the measurable changes in production are isolated effects of the performance intervention and incorporate the effects into the ROI calculations (Fusch, 2008).

After analyzing the questionnaires and measurable changes in production, you can convert the isolated effects of the intervention/training strategy into a quantifiable monetary value and apply them in the ROI model (Fusch, 2008).

Reduction in Customer Complaints, Customer Callbacks, and so on as Applicable

Bartel (2000) conducted an analytical study of 500 ROI studies. One example she highlighted was measuring the reduction in customer complaints and callbacks after a performance improvement initiative. She found that the savings in time was a good measurable indicator of the business benefit.

Expanding on the time savings resulting from the reduction in customer complaints after a training initiative, Bartel (2000) noted in a warehouse study that the performance professionals used the reduction in supervisor time dealing with customer complaints on the phone. In the particular warehouse study, the savings of time was substantial. Multiplying the time savings by the supervisor wage/benefit package provided a good measurement of the initiative's impact on the business. Indeed, production time savings × annual wage package = monetary value per participant (Fusch, 2008).

Reduction in the Amount of Time Needed to Perform a Task

One strategy is to determine how much faster an employee can perform a task after a performance initiative. Fusch (2008) developed a strategy where a paper manufacturer could determine the savings in pay to individuals spread across the production plant by multiplying the complete pay package (salary and benefits) by the time saved to determine the business benefit. Fusch's premise was that if people can perform faster, they can perform more work, and this will lead to increased productivity or less cost for employees. From a perspective of valuing people, Fusch argued that organizational leaders should strive to expand markets rather than undertake a reduction in force because of performance improvement. Doing so further increases the business's mission to acquire wealth and gain additional capital to grow and prosper and do so in Valuing Ways.

Reduction in Scrap/Waste

Using cost reduction to measure the effects of the performance intervention through scrape/waste reduction requires assessing the value of waste. Indeed, this is one method to isolate the cost of scrap/waste by the increased production in marketable goods. Another strategy suggests that a manufacturing facility measure scrape/waste reduction and implement a tracking system throughout the facility to calculate the monetary cost of waste from maintenance parts to raw materials to finished product. Such a tracking system may identify higher waste areas and point out the need for additional performance interventions.

Step 3: Calculate the Total Cost of a Performance Intervention

After isolating the effects of the performance intervention, through either increased production or waste reduction, and converting the effects to a monetary value, you can calculate the total performance intervention cost. Depending on an organization's accounting procedures, different cost categories must be calculated to identify performance intervention costs.

As shown in Figure A.7, these costs include the fixed cost (performance administration costs, facility and administration fixed costs), intervention design and development cost (or purchase cost if obtained from an external vendor), delivery cost (performance/learning personnel, materials, equipment, outside facilities), and wages and benefits for participants if there will be time away from performing regular activities (or overtime wages and benefits to cover for people away from performing regular activities).

Of the different cost, the fixed cost most often provides challenges. As shown in Figure A.8, the fixed cost includes the performance administration personnel, capital expenses such as equipment used for performance and learning interventions, operational budget such as office supplies, and facility and utility costs.

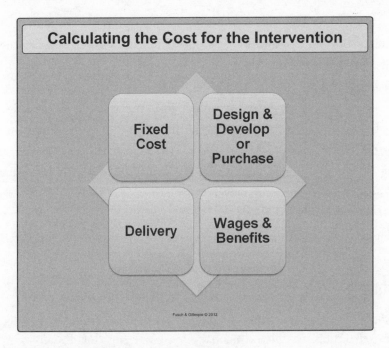

Figure A.7 Calculating the cost of the intervention

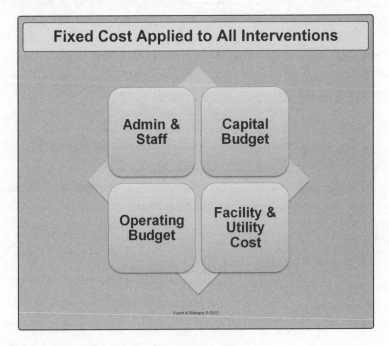

Figure A.8 Fixed costs applied to all interventions

Sometimes identifying a specific fixed cost requires thinking outside the box. The following case study demonstrates how Fusch (2008) calculated the training cost for a paper mill that had some specific challenges. After the individual costs are calculated, the challenge becomes attributing a specific fixed cost to a specific intervention, such as a training program or department briefing to roll out a new job aid. The strategy that we suggest is to calculate the time spent rolling out interventions, such as the hours of training during the previous years, to get a trend analysis. Using the trend analysis, divide the total fixed cost by the hours for the interventions, such as training, to identify a per-hour fixed cost.

Intervention Administration Fixed Costs Case Study

This case study examines a training ROI project for a paper mill. Fusch (2008) calculated each hour of training that the training department provided (which would be updated each year to provide a precise cost for each training course), the training course cost for each individual course, and the wages of course participants paid while they were in training. The training administration costs were fixed costs that applied to all the company's training initiatives. As with many industrial facilities, calculating the mill's training administration costs was complicated by issues with the age of the plant and the separation of training facility cost from the manufacturing operations cost, and the sharing of the training facility with the human resources department. The challenge began with assigning costs to the training facility. This was amplified by the fact that not only did the mill's training department share a building with the human resources department, but the electrical utility costs were not separated from the total industrial plant utility purchases. Furthermore, the building was owned outright and had long since been depreciated.

To calculate the building costs, Fusch analyzed the building blueprints. He calculated that the training department occupied 56 percent of the building, and the human resources department occupied 44 percent. By multiplying the building costs by 56 percent, Fusch was able to determine the training department's building costs.

The water and natural gas costs were charged separately to the building and therefore required a simple input into the expense equation. The mill did not identify a cost for the building or for the electrical usage separate from the mill. Considering that an expense was not identified for the building rent or depreciation, it was logical that if the human resources and training departments did not occupy the building, it could be rented for office space and produce rental revenue (which in turn could be used to identify a cost). Moreover, if the training department rented a similar building outside the plant, there would be a calculable cost. Therefore, Fusch calculated the rental value by surveying commercial realtors to find equivalent buildings in the area.

The electrical costs presented another interesting dilemma. Through inquiries with electrical designers, Fusch discovered a general per-square-foot electrical calculation for comparable facilities and was able to determine an annual electrical cost.

In addition to the training facility costs, the mill's training budget included training department wages and benefits, rental fees/ leases on office equipment, office furniture, computer software, procurement card expenses, travel expenses, telephone costs, and consultant fees. Note that these costs reflected the fixed training administration budget and excluded the specific costs assigned to individual training courses.

After calculating the sum of the total fixed administrative training costs, Fusch divided this sum by the total annual course training hours (calculated from an average of previous years). This provided an administrative training cost per hour of instruction.

In this ROI model, the total course costs included the fixed administrative costs, the specific training course costs (purchase cost, consultants, trainers' wages, course development time, in-house experts' development time, trainer class prep time, course manuals, miscellaneous materials), and the wages and benefits of course participants.

After identifying all of the training cost, Fusch (2008) calculated the total cost and inserted it into the ROI model. The calculation required adding the total costs of the training administration per instructional hour, the training course cost for each individual course, and the wages and benefits of course participants that were paid while they were in training.

After you calculate the fixed-cost-per-hour rate, multiply the fixed cost by the number of hours planned for a specific intervention. Then add the fixed cost, intervention design and development cost (or purchase cost), delivery cost, and wages and benefits for participants if they will take time off from performing their regular activities (or overtime wages and benefits to replace people while they are away from performing their regular activities).

Step 4: Calculate the Net Benefit of a Performance Intervention

The fourth step in the ROI process is to subtract the total intervention project/program costs from the total program benefits to determine the training program's net benefit. In this calculation, the total course costs are subtracted from the monetary value of the effects of the training program to equal the net benefit.

Step 5: Calculate the ROI

The final step in the ROI process is to calculate the ROI. Figure A.9 mathematically depicts the ROI process. You take the monetary value of the effects of performance intervention and subtract the cost of performance intervention to get the net benefit of performance intervention. Then you divide the net benefit of performance intervention by the total cost of performance intervention to calculate the ROI. Because we are used to looking at the ROI in percentages, you multiply the ROI by 100 to calculate the ROI percentage, which we call ROI %.

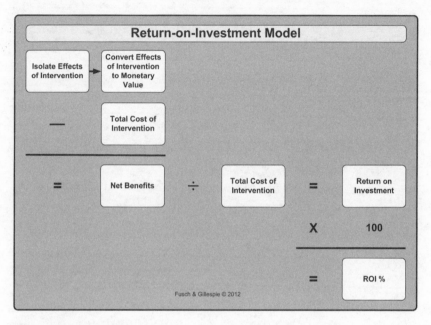

Figure A.9 ROI model

Summary

In addition to writing about ROI strategies, Fusch and Gillespie frequently work with organizations on performance assessment through determining an ROI for a performance initiative. We frequently work with performance improvement associations (ISPI, ASTD, SHRM) and for-profit and nonprofit organizations. We offer workshops on performance improvement strategies (maximizing employee performance), Work/Life Approaches, and practical ROI strategies. Moreover, we argue that not only does conducting an ROI evaluate the impact of a performance initiative (Work/Life Approach) on the desired end results (see Figure A.10), but it also can justify your job and illuminate your contribution to the organization.

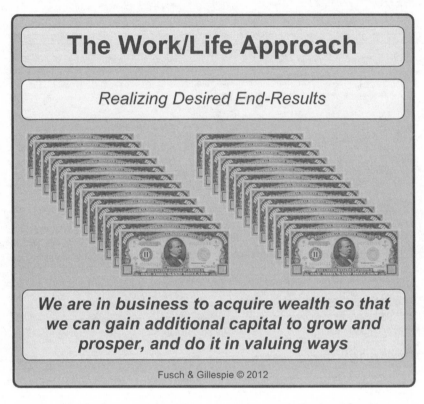

Figure A.10 The Work/Life Approach to realizing the desired end results

B

The Authors and Their Perspectives

This book is about creating performance cultures in the workplace. It describes theoretical models for human competence and performance improvement and includes practical how-tos; performance analysis, gap analysis, measurement, and evaluation; and powerful Work/Life Approaches.

From a cultural performance perspective, it is important to realize that each organization has an individual and specific culture that is influenced by its own norms, rituals, rites, and people. To look at a workplace culture is to look at it from the perspective of a cultural anthropologist learning from within the culture and sharing with those outside the culture. Although this is a conceptually rich and practical book on performance culture and innovative initiatives, it is important that we, the authors, share our own perspectives and adhere to the Rule of the Cultural Anthropologist and be open about where we stand.

We believe that the performance improvement model and the Work/Life Approach speak for themselves. Making these Working Beliefs a part of our daily focus for continuous improvement at home, in business, and in our public lives has been a worthy endeavor. We continuously work to get better at implementing these ideas. These conceptual and practical ideas are an amalgamation of our careers in working with organizations to help them realize desired end results. Furthermore, these ideas also come from our personal mission to live in a better world. They are strongly influenced by our social, economic, political, and religious beliefs, which were the foundation for developing the Work/Life Approach.

The primary reason for this book was our faith in God, his teachings in the Old Testament of the Bible, and the teachings of Jesus Christ in the New Testament. We acknowledge our religious beliefs because they are the foundation for our social, economic, and political beliefs. We expect that as you read this book, you may have found a kindred spirit. Some may reject the idea of our Christian beliefs, some may say so what, some may have different beliefs—so be it.

The performance improvement techniques and Work/Life Approach are so powerful and valid that they stand on their own. Use them and enjoy them. If you elect not to use them, please thoroughly consider the alternatives and the end result if you elect not to use them.

About the Authors

Gene E. Fusch, PhD
Current Affiliations

- Organizational leadership and performance consultant
- President of Gene Fusch and Associates
- Contributing member of the brain trust at Intrepid Learning
- Contributing faculty methodologist at Walden University's Doctorate in Business Administration program
- Doctoral Committee chair for the Northcentral University School of Business and Technology Management

Leadership and Management

Dr. Fusch's career has spanned both business and education. He has conducted research on performance effectiveness and linked theory to real-world practice, as well as assisted business school students in reaching their educational goals. As a leadership and organizational performance consultant, he has helped many organizations with performance improvement initiatives. His clients have included Alcoa-Intalco Works, ARCO, AT&T Cable Systems, Boeing Airplane Company, British Petroleum, Dri-Eaz Products, Georgia Pacific Corporation, Hexcel Interiors, Multi-Care Healthcare Systems, National Transportation Training Directors, TOSCO Refinery, Washington State Department of Transportation, Whatcom EMS, US West Communications, and Yahoo!.

Personal Interests

To balance his professional life with his faith and personal endeavors, after raising their children, Dr. Fusch and his wife designed and built a home on the Hood Canal in Washington State. Today his hobbies include boat building, sailing, and fishing the waters of Puget Sound, the San Juan Islands, the Gulf Islands, and the Inland Passage of British Columbia.

Contact Information

gfusch@gfa.biz

Richard C. Gillespie
Current Affiliations

- Organizational leadership and management consultant
- President of Work/Life Systems International
- Chief operations officer for Salty's Waterfront Seafood Restaurants
- Master of the obvious (MOTO)

Leadership and Management Experience

Gillespie helps organizations realize their desired end results with leadership audits, change management initiatives, and financial turn-arounds. Gerry Kingen, founder of Red Robin and Salty's restaurant chains and current CEO of Salty's, credits Gillespie as "master of the obvious" for his ability to provide succinct and straight forward Work/Life Approaches to resolve complex business needs. Some of his clients have included Lutheran Universities and Colleges, U.S. Forest Service, *Weyerhaeuser*, and John L Scott Real Estate Corporation. In addition to consulting, Gillespie has served as president for Dri-Eaz Products, and chief operations officer for Salty's Waterfront Seafood Restaurants.

Personal Interests

After an extensive career as a problem solver and organizational leadership and management consultant, Gillespie is actively helping organizations realize their desired end results. Gillespie and his wife enjoy getting involved in their community and church, as well as spending valuable time with their children and grandchildren.

Contact Information

rcgi@frontier.com

References

APA. (2009). *Publication manual of the American Psychological Association.* (6th ed.). Washington, DC: American Psychological Association.

Bartel, A. P. (2000). Measuring the employer's return on investments in training: *Evidence from the literature. Industrial Relations, 39*(3), 502-523.

Becker, G. S. (1993). Human capital: A theoretical and empirical analysis with special reference to education (3rd ed.). Chicago: University of Chicago Press.

Binder, C. (1995). Promoting human performance technology innovation: A return to our natural science roots. *Performance Improvement Quarterly, 8*(2), 95-113.

Bowles, S., & Gintes, H. (1975). The problem with human capital theory--A—Marxian critique. *American Economic Review, 65*(2), 74-82.

Carroll, A. B., & Buchholtz, A. K. (2009). *Business & society: Ethics and stakeholder management.* (7th ed.). Mason, OH: South-Western Cengage Learning.

Covey, S. R. (2004). *The 7 habits of highly effective people.* New York: Fireside/Simon and Schuster.

Denzin, N. K. (1970). *The research act in sociology.* Chicago: Aldine.

Denzin, N. K. (2009). *The research act: A theoretical introduction to sociological methods.* (Reprint, 1970). New York, N.Y.: Aldine Transaction.

Edmund, M., & Juran, J. M. (2008). The architect of quality: Joseph M. Juran 1904-2008. *Quality Progress, 41*(4), 20-25. Retrieved from: http://asq.org/qualityprogress/index.html.

Fusch, G. E. (1999). Organizational transition. *Performance Improvement Journal, 38*(10), 18.

Fusch, G. E. (2001a). Work/Life and the workplace—An ethnographic case study of a high performance working environment. Doctoral Dissertation, Southern Illinois University, Carbondale.

Fusch, G. E. (2001b, July). Review of Meister, Jeanne C. (1998). Corporate universities: Lessons in building a world-class work force. (Rev. ed.). *Education Review*. Retrieved from http://www.edrev.info/reviews/rev129.htm.

Fusch, G. E. (2008). What happens when the ROI model does not fit? *Performance Improvement Quarterly, 14*(4), 60-76. doi:10.1111/j.1937-8327.2001. tb00230.x.

Gilbert, T. F. (2007). *Human competence: Engineering worthy performance,* (3rd ed.). Hoboken, NJ: Pfeiffer.

Gillespie, R. C. (1992). *Managing is everybody's business.* Port Ludlow, WA: Olympic Publishing.

Hale, J. (1998). Evaluation: It's time to go beyond levels, 1, 2, 3, and 4. *Performance Improvement, 37*(2), 30-34.

Kelly, G. A. (1955). *The psychology of personal constructs.* New York: Norton.

Kirkpatrick, D. L. (2006). *Evaluating training programs: The four levels.* (3rd ed.). San Francisco: Berrett-Koehler.

Likert, R. (1967). *The human organization: Its management and value.* New York: McGraw Hill.

Mager, R. F. & Pipe, P. (1997). *Analyzing performance problems or you really oughta wanna* (3rd ed.). Atlanta, GA: The Center for Effective Performance.

Maslow, A. H. (1970). *Motivation and personality* (2nd ed.). New York: Harper and Row.

Mathieu, J. E., & Martineau, J. W. (1997). Individual and situational influences on training motivation. In J. K. Ford, S. W. J. Kozlowski, K. Kraiger, E. Salas, & M. S. Teachout (Eds.), *Improving training effectiveness in work organizations* (pp. 193-221). Mahwah, NJ: Lawrence Erlbaum Associates.

Mayo, E. (1949). Hawthorne and the Western Electric Company. In D. S. Pugh (Ed.). (1971), *Organizational Theory* (pp. 215-229). London: Cox & Wyman Ltd.

Morgan, G. (1986). *Images of organization*. Newbury Park, California: Sage.

National Institute of Standards and Technology (2011). *Baldrige performance excellence program*. Retrieved from: http://www.nist.gov/baldrige/about/performance_excellence.cfm.

Nonaka, I. & Takeuchi, H. (1995). *The knowledge-creating company—how Japanese companies create the dynamics on innovation*. New York and Oxford: Oxford University Press.

Phillips, J. J. (1997). *Return on investment: In training and performance improvement programs*. Houston, TX: Gulf Publishing.

Phillips, J. J., & Phillips, P. P. (2011). *Measuring ROI in learning and development*. Alexandria, VA: American Society for Training & Development.

Senge, P. (1990). *The fifth discipline: the art and practice of the learning organization*. New York: Doubleday-Currency.

Stolovitch, H. D., & Maurice, J. G. (1998). Calculating the return on investment in training: A critical analysis and a case study. *Performance Improvement, 37*(8), 9-20.

Stolovitch, H. D., & Keeps, E. J. (eds.). (2004). *Performance ain't training*. Alexandria, VA: ASTD Press.

Stolovitch, H. D., & Keeps, E. J. (eds.). (2006). *Beyond performance ain't training fieldbook*. Alexandria, VA: ASTD Press.

Taylor, F. W. (1911). *The principles of scientific management* (Reprint 1998). Mineola, NY: Dover.

Vroom, V. H. (1959). *Some personality determinants of the effects of participation*. Engle Cliffs, NJ: Prentice-Hall.

Vroom, V. H. (1964). *Work and motivation*. New York: John Wiley.

Index

FINANCIAL TIMES

In an increasingly competitive world, it is quality
of thinking that gives an edge—an idea that opens new
doors, a technique that solves a problem, or an insight
that simply helps make sense of it all.

We work with leading authors in the various arenas
of business and finance to bring cutting-edge thinking
and best-learning practices to a global market.

It is our goal to create world-class print publications
and electronic products that give readers
knowledge and understanding that can then be
applied, whether studying or at work.

To find out more about our business
products, you can visit us at www.ftpress.com.